D1569932

Prince
Harry

Prince Harry

By: Cherese Cartlidge

LUCENT BOOKS

A part of Gale, Cengage Learning

GALE
CENGAGE Learning·

Detroit • New York • San Francisco • New Haven, Conn • Waterville, Maine • London

LIBRARY OF CONGRESS CATALOGING-IN-PUBLICATION DATA

Cartlidge, Cherese.
  Prince Harry / by Cherese Cartlidge.
    p. cm. -- (People in the news)
  Includes bibliographical references and index.
  ISBN 978-1-4205-0760-7 (hardcover)
  1. Henry, Prince, grandson of Elizabeth II, Queen of Great Britain, 1984---
Juvenile literature. 2. Princes--Great Britain--Biography--Juvenile literature.
  I. Title.
    DA591.A45H4633 2012
    941.086092--dc23
    [B]
                                                        2012024944

Lucent Books
27500 Drake Rd
Farmington Hills MI 48331

ISBN-13: 978-1-4205-0760-7
ISBN-10: 1-4205-0760-5

Printed in the United States of America
1 2 3 4 5 6 7 16 15 14 13 12

Contents

Fame and celebrity are alluring. People are drawn to those who walk in fame's spotlight, whether they are known for great accomplishments or for notorious deeds. The lives of the famous pique public interest and attract attention, perhaps because their experiences seem in some ways so different from, yet in other ways so similar to, our own.

Newspapers, magazines, and television regularly capitalize on this fascination with celebrity by running profiles of famous people. For example, television programs such as *Entertainment Tonight* devote all their programming to stories about entertainment and entertainers. Magazines such as *People* fill their pages with stories of the private lives of famous people. Even newspapers, newsmagazines, and television news frequently delve into the lives of well-known personalities. Despite the number of articles and programs, few provide more than a superficial glimpse at their subjects.

Lucent's People in the News series offers young readers a deeper look into the lives of today's newsmakers, the influences that have shaped them, and the impact they have had in their fields of endeavor and on other people's lives. The subjects of the series hail from many disciplines and walks of life. They include authors, musicians, athletes, political leaders, entertainers, entrepreneurs, and others who have made a mark on modern life and who, in many cases, will continue to do so for years to come.

These biographies are more than factual chronicles. Each book emphasizes the contributions, accomplishments, or deeds that have brought fame or notoriety to the individual and shows how that person has influenced modern life. Authors portray their subjects in a realistic, unsentimental light. For example, Bill Gates—cofounder of the software giant Microsoft—has been instrumental in making personal computers the most vital tool of the modern age. Few dispute his business savvy, his perseverance, or his technical expertise, yet critics say he is ruthless in his dealings with competitors and driven more by his desire to maintain Microsoft's dominance in the computer industry than by an interest in furthering technology.

In these books, young readers will encounter inspiring stories about real people who achieved success despite enormous obstacles. Oprah Winfrey—one of the most powerful, most watched, and wealthiest women in television history—spent the first six years of her life in the care of her grandparents while her unwed mother sought work and a better life elsewhere. Her adolescence was colored by pregnancy at age fourteen, rape, and sexual abuse.

Each author documents and supports his or her work with an array of primary and secondary source quotations taken from diaries, letters, speeches, and interviews. All quotes are footnoted to show readers exactly how and where biographers derive their information and provide guidance for further research. The quotations enliven the text by giving readers eyewitness views of the life and accomplishments of each person covered in the People in the News series.

In addition, each book in the series includes photographs, annotated bibliographies, timelines, and comprehensive indexes. For both the casual reader and the student researcher, the People in the News series offers insight into the lives of today's newsmakers—people who shape the way we live, work, and play in the modern age.

The Maverick Prince

Prince Harry of England is the second son of two of the most well-known people to live in the modern era. His father is Charles, the Prince of Wales, who will one day take over as the monarch, or ruler, of England. His mother is the late Diana, Princess of Wales, who came from the aristocratic Spencer family. Harry has only one sibling—his older brother, William, who will one day succeed their father as king of England.

Harry's full name is Henry Charles David Albert—"Harry" is his nickname, and like the rest of his father's family, he does not actually have a last name. Although the family name is considered to be Windsor, and Harry is part of the royal House of Windsor, the name is not used as a surname by members of the British royal family. Instead, Harry uses the name of the area over which his father is prince: Wales. He is often referred to as either Prince Henry of Wales or Prince Harry of Wales. Currently a captain in the British Army, he is known in the military as Captain Harry Wales.

Prince Harry's grandmother is Queen Elizabeth II, the current queen of England. Prince Charles is next in line to the British throne, followed by his eldest son, William. Harry is third in the line of succession to the throne, after his father and brother; consequently, he is also third in line as Supreme Governor of the Church of England.

The Heir and the Spare

When Princess Diana gave birth to Harry, the second son of Prince Charles, in 1984, the world quickly began referring to the princes William and Harry as "the heir and the spare." Charles and William

Prince Harry, center, stands with his brother, Prince William, and grandmother, Queen Elizabeth, on a balcony at Buckingham Palace in 2009. The queen's oldest son, Prince Charles, is the heir apparent to the British throne.

are both eldest sons, and William is heir to the throne after his father. Harry is the "spare" son, who can step in as heir to the throne if anything should happen to his brother, William.

Because Charles is the eldest son of a reigning monarch, he is first in line to the throne, and his place as future king cannot be usurped by the birth of another male heir. This is called an heir apparent. William is second in line to the throne, and it is his duty to take over as king after his father. Because he is Charles's eldest son, William's place as future king also cannot be usurped, making him also an heir apparent. As the second son of Prince Charles, Harry is the heir presumptive—meaning that his place in the line of succession can change. He has been third in line to the throne from the moment he was born, but should William produce a child, Harry would then become fourth in line.

Growing up, Harry was in a similar position to another second son: his uncle, Prince Andrew, who is the second son of Elizabeth and is Charles's younger brother. Andrew was second in line to the throne until he was twenty-two, when William was born. Andrew then became third in line, and, after Harry's birth, fourth.

Officially, Harry's royal purpose is to take William's place as king, should the need arise. That is why he is often called the spare heir. If William were to die before their father, and before producing a child of his own, Harry would step in as second in line to the throne—and would become an heir apparent as well. On the other hand, should both Harry's father and brother die without William having produced an heir, then Harry would become the next king of England. Either way, because of Harry, the monarchy in the form of the House of Windsor would survive even if something were to happen to both the first and second in line to the throne.

"Three Heartbeats Away"

Being the second son meant that Harry often felt like he was unimportant while he was growing up. He was not the one who was going to become king—William was. The situation also led to Harry feeling like nothing he did mattered as much as what William did. As a teen and young adult, Harry therefore engaged in wild behavior that was often the subject of sensational headlines. He drank at a young age, experimented with marijuana, threw temper tantrums, and had several romps with young women. He does not have the same heavy responsibilities as William, a fact that has allowed him to be more reckless and wild than his brother. He has more freedom to behave the way he wants because, as Harry explained, "William's got—well, we've both got our lives set out, but I think he's got his life *really* set out."[1]

Like the rest of the British royal family, Prince Harry is recognized throughout the world, wherever he goes, and has been all his life. In fact, it is rare that he can just blend in when he is in public. He is constantly followed and photographed, even when he is trying to relax. Yet for Harry, the pressure is off to behave in ways befitting a future king. Richard Kay, a columnist for the British tabloid the *Daily Mail* who was also a close friend of Diana's, says, "He wants to be noticed, I think he enjoys being noticed, but I think he also loves the fact that it doesn't matter what he does because, in a way, he's not important. Although serious people will tell you, 'but he's only three heartbeats away from the throne.' Well, he is, but no one expects him seriously to actually reach it."[2]

Although Harry remains modest, he is also realistic about his status as a member of the royal family. "I am who I am, though I believe I'm no one special."[3] Harry was always an active and mischievous child, and after the divorce of his parents and death of his mother, his rebellious behavior only increased. Although today he seems to have outgrown his childish past and matured into a respected young man with a career in the military and concern and compassion for those less fortunate than himself, he remains something of a maverick, insisting on doing things his own way.

Chapter 1

The Spare Heir

Prince Harry was a bright and precocious child. He grew up surrounded by loving parents, a protective big brother, and doting grandparents. Although Harry and his brother, William, were both royalty, their parents made every effort to make their childhood as "normal" as possible. Harry's parents also strove to ensure that their second son never felt like he came second in their eyes. As a result, Harry developed an especially close relationship with each of his parents, as well as with his brother.

The World Welcomes Prince Harry

His Royal Highness Prince Henry Charles David Albert of Wales was born on September 15, 1984. He was delivered at St. Mary's Hospital in London by the same doctor who had delivered his brother, William, two years earlier. His father, Prince Charles, was in the delivery room when Harry arrived that afternoon. Newborn Harry had light blue eyes and a little bit of reddish hair. Immediately after Harry's birth, Charles called his mother, the queen of England, to tell her the news. Then he drove back to Kensington Palace to tell William about his new baby brother.

Harry's birth was announced in headlines around the world. The Prince and Princess of Wales had not only produced a male heir to the throne in William, they had now produced a second son who could take William's place as king if necessary, thereby ensuring the continuation of the House of Windsor. To celebrate the birth of the "spare heir," as Harry is often called, numerous

Prince Charles and Princess Diana leave St. Mary's Hospital with their newborn son, Prince Harry, in September 1984. Because he was an heir to the British throne, Harry's birth made headlines around the world.

commemorative souvenirs were issued, including china mugs, thimbles, china dolls, tea towels, and postcards. Tons of presents from well-wishers poured in for Harry and his parents, including flowers, balloons, telegrams, and toys. A number of high-profile people sent special gifts; singer Barry Manilow sent a miniature antique baby-grand piano, while pop star Michael Jackson sent a toy stuffed monkey and a card.

By all accounts, Harry was an easy baby to take care of. Charles said that baby Harry was "extraordinarily good, sleeps marvelously and eats well." He added that Harry was "the one with the gentle nature,"[4] whereas William was the boisterous one. Indeed, Harry was a quiet baby. At his christening, which took place at Windsor Castle on December 21 when he was three months old, Harry cried for only two or three minutes when the Archbishop of Canterbury sprinkled him with holy water. "He was as quiet as a mouse throughout the rest,"[5] recalled one of the choirboys.

A Special Relationship with William

Growing up with an older brother can make any young boy sometimes feel like he comes in second, and this situation was doubly so for Harry, whose big brother was slated to become king. As a child Harry sometimes felt like he was invisible or did not matter, because people would make a fuss over his brother while ignoring him. But both his parents worked hard to make sure he never felt like he came second to William in their eyes, particularly Diana. During her pregnancy, for example, she went shopping for new baby clothes and toys at Harrods department store, even though Charles suggested they just use William's hand-me-downs.

One of the ways Diana tried to make Harry feel important was by involving him in William's life—and William in his.

Just over a year old, Harry, right, plays at the piano with William at their home in Kensington Palace in October 1985. The brothers have had a close relationship since they were very young.

While she was pregnant Diana encouraged William to bond with the new baby by touching her tummy. When the two-year-old William first met Harry on the morning after his birth, he kissed Harry's forehead and described his new brother as "the most beautiful thing I have ever seen."[6] This affection for his baby brother continued after Harry was brought home from the hospital. "Harry was his favorite toy,"[7] Diana confessed. She recalled family time when Harry was an infant: "William spends the entire time pouring an endless supply of hugs and kisses on Harry and we are hardly allowed near."[8] As they got older, Diana always made sure Harry was included in William's activities and was in the picture whenever his brother was photographed.

Partly as a result of their mother's efforts to involve them in each other's lives, Harry and William became extremely close. They were—and still are—each other's best friends and share a very tight bond. William was very protective of his little brother, and Harry, in turn, worshipped his big brother and tried to emulate him. This was sometimes very cute, but other times it could be difficult; if William ran around a room screaming at the top of his lungs, Harry would do the same thing.

As a young child Harry would often climb into bed with William during the night. He could not bear to be apart from his brother, and so it came as a terrible blow to Harry when he was told shortly after his first birthday that William was starting nursery school and would be gone all morning. Harry burst into tears at the news, and two mornings a week he was inconsolable when William went off to school. Eventually, Diana let Harry come along when she drove William to school so he could spend a few extra minutes with his big brother.

Harry and William both loved all kinds of physical activities, including swimming, skiing, tennis, polo, and rugby. At an early age, it became obvious that even though William was very athletic, Harry was better at sports. "The sporting star of the family is definitely Harry, and it always has been," says journalist Ingrid Seward. "And that used to really irritate William, because he would see his younger brother better on the skis than he was. And Harry was fearless."[9]

A Normal Childhood

Both Charles and Diana were devoted parents, and they cut back on their royal duties after the birth of their sons to spend more time with their children. They agreed that both boys should have as "normal" a childhood as possible, and Diana in particular took special care to make this happen. She made sure they had plenty of chances to play with ordinary kids in a normal social setting. She also dressed them in regular, everyday clothes such as jeans, sweatshirts, striped T-shirts, and baseball caps, rather than the matching suits or traditional sailor outfits worn by the children of many royals.

Most of all, Diana wanted Harry and William to have fun and enjoy their childhood before they became adults and took on the heavy responsibilities that come with their royal positions. She made sure they got to enjoy fast-food hamburgers at restaurants

Harry takes a ride on his pony in 1991. Despite the fact that their family was royalty and very wealthy, Charles and Diana tried to make sure the boys had as normal a childhood as possible.

like McDonald's and Burger King. She never asked for or accepted any special treatment when she took the boys there, and she insisted they wait in line like everybody else.

Diana wanted her sons to be as normal as possible and so taught them not to take advantage of people because they were royal. Yet the fact remained that Harry's family was very wealthy. Their country home boasted nine main bedrooms, four reception rooms, a nursery wing, and staff quarters. Servants included butlers, a housekeeper, a chef, a nanny, and several personal attendants. Because she could afford to buy her sons whatever they wanted, Diana showered them with gifts like TV sets, computers and computer games, and a Sony PlayStation. Harry and William grew up with all the latest high-tech gadgets, and like most kids their age, they loved playing computer games and had a large collection of all the latest games. The boys also had their own Shetland ponies, as well as a scaled-down replica of a Jaguar automobile that they drove around the countryside at 15 miles per hour (24kph).

At Home with the Royals

Harry's family had two main residences, which they split their time between. Their home in London was at Kensington Palace, which was built in the early seventeenth century. The family's apartment at Kensington had a rooftop garden, which the family often used for barbeques. The boys shared an attic room that was converted into a nursery featuring furniture with hand-painted animals and cartoon characters. The big room had yellow walls filled with bookcases and cabinets for toys. It also had a wooden rocking horse that was a gift from Nancy Reagan, wife of then U.S. president Ronald Reagan. The boys ate their meals in the nursery, and Diana often joined them. She and Charles would also attend tea parties in the nursery that William put on, while Harry would scream and run around.

Their country home, the place where Harry truly felt happiest, was Highgrove House. The three-story, nine-bedroom house, built in 1796, is located in 348 wooded acres (141ha) about two hours' drive west of London. Some of Harry's earliest memories are of

Charles and Diana pose with Harry, left, and William at Highgrove House, the family's country home, in 1986. Harry has spoken of his fond memories of time spent at Highgrove when he was a child.

Making Harry Count

In spite of his parents' efforts, Harry often felt like he did not matter because it was William who would become king and not him. But his mother wanted to make sure Harry felt important, too. Richard Kay, a British journalist who was also a close friend of Diana's, explains:

> She worried, because he was the number two, that he would be the one who would be overlooked. Everyone would come to William; William was the one they were grooming for the future. And it was one of the reasons why Diana used to say ... that she wanted to involve Harry in William's life. And it carries on to this day. William rarely does photo calls on his own. Harry is always drawn into those, because she didn't want him to be constantly overlooked—"Oh, he's the spare, he doesn't count." She wanted him to count.

Quoted in *Harry: The Mysterious Prince.* DVD. Directed by Alan Scales. London: BBC Worldwide/Infinity, 2005.

playing in the walled garden within the grounds of Highgrove. Like the rest of his immediate family, young Harry had a great love of the outdoors and of animals. The family went to Highgrove as often as possible. Charles wanted to pass on his love of rural activities to the boys, which included teaching them to hunt and shoot.

The boys also learned to ride horses at Highgrove. Since William is two years older, he learned this skill long before Harry. William had two ponies at Highgrove, Smokey and Trigger. When he was about three or four years old he would be led around on them, with Harry watching from the sidelines. As a toddler, Harry would sometimes get to sit in the saddle with William while the pony stood still, but Harry was too small to actually ride it and cried when he was taken off the pony.

He and William loved exploring the grounds at Highgrove. The house is surrounded by an estate that includes the 900-acre (364ha) Highgrove Farm. The boys helped care for the rabbits and guinea pigs and got to watch lambs being sheared. A favorite game was to run into a farm field shouting at the top of their lungs, and make all the cows and sheep run away. The weekends spent at Highgrove were happy, carefree times for the young family.

"One Long Laugh"

Harry had a close relationship with both parents and spent a great deal of time with each of them. Unlike many other royals before her, Diana was a very hands-on mother who insisted on doing things like driving the boys to school herself. Ken Wharfe, a police bodyguard who protected Diana and her two sons for seven years, recalls that Diana never missed a single day unless it was absolutely unavoidable. "The opportunity to talk through their school day with 'Mummy' on the short car journey from

Diana, in the back row, rides with William, left front, and Harry, right front, on Disney World's Splash Mountain in 1993. The princes remember their trip to Disney World with their mother as one of their favorite vacations.

Kensington Palace to both kindergarten at Jane Mynors's and pre-prep [pre-preparatory school] at the Wetherby School was an invaluable time for the boys," he says. "Both William and Harry loved this aspect of their mother's involvement."[10]

Indeed, Diana was very involved in her sons' lives and loved to play and laugh along with them. The boys loved to play all sorts of sports, and both were very athletic. Their mother often joined them. She would be goalkeeper for their football (soccer) matches on the lawn at Kensington Palace. When Harry was eight, he attended a cowboys-and-Indians-themed tea party with his mother and brother that was hosted by the king of Greece. Diana dressed up in a cowgirl outfit, and Harry and William wore cowboy outfits. Diana also took them to Disney World in 1993, which was one of their favorite vacations ever. "When the boys were very young," said Diana, "I just remember life being one long laugh whenever they were there."[11]

Both boys adored their mother and loved spending hours watching TV with her, especially the British comedy *Mr. Bean*. They also loved to tickle their mother until she collapsed on the floor in a heap of giggles. "I tickle back," she said, "but it's two of them and one of me and I am so much more ticklish than they are anyway. It's not fair, but of course that doesn't bother them in the slightest."[12]

As a young boy, Harry was somewhat insecure in his attachment to his mother. Writer Judy Wade described him as "a terribly affectionate little boy, always wrapped around his mother, sneaking into her bed early in the morning for a cuddle."[13] Harry tended to cling to Diana as a child and needed lots of reassurance from her. "If they were in a room together, Harry would sit almost on top of Diana in his anxiety to be close to her,"[14] says Ingrid Seward. A thumbsucker, Harry did not give up the self-comforting habit until he was eleven years old.

Harry and the Prince of Wales

Harry always had a good relationship with his father, too. As a little boy he spent a great deal of time at Charles's side in the garden at Highgrove, digging holes in the dirt for hours. "Harry loves animals and plants," Charles once said. "I tell him all about them and say they have feelings, too, and mustn't be hurt."[15] Harry had his own tool kit, which contained a child-sized trowel, fork, and rake. Just like his father, he would also talk to the plants—and sometimes to himself. Harry's childish, one-sided conversations would cause his father to have to suppress laughter. Harry adored spending these summer afternoons with his father. He especially loved the evenings, when they would sit on a garden bench with

Blue, Brown, and Pink Grannies

When Harry and William were young children, Diana taught them their own special way to refer to British money. Because the queen's face appears on British currency (called pounds), the boys called each bill a "granny." Different denominations of British currency are different colors; therefore, the princes called a five-pound note a "blue

The face of Queen Elizabeth II is on the fifty-pound note, called the "pink granny" by young Harry and William.

granny," a ten-pound note a "brown granny," and a fifty-pound note a "pink granny." The boys loved having their own unique way of referring to money, and whenever Diana asked them how much spending money they needed, they would always ask for a pink granny. This private way of referring to pound notes continued into their adulthood. Although many royals do not carry cash, leaving bar tabs or restaurant checks for others to pay, Harry and William always make sure they have enough grannies on hand to pay their own way.

a bottle of orange squash [similar to lemonade, but made from oranges] after hours of digging. The two talked as the sun set and stayed on the bench until it got too dark to see.

Like Diana, Charles was a very hands-on parent who loved to spend time with both boys. He played games with them and took them horseback riding. When they were old enough, he took them hunting. Charles also read to both boys when they were young. A favorite book was C.S. Lewis's *The Lion, the Witch, and the Wardrobe*. As Harry got older and began to learn to read, Charles would listen patiently while his young son sounded out the words in the book. Harry inherited his father's love of reading. Charles would take him into his personal library at Highgrove in the evenings, and Harry would look around for a new book to read. One of Harry's favorite authors while he was growing up was the American horror novelist Stephen King.

Harry especially loved spending time with his father at Balmoral Castle in Scotland. He and his father would take long walks in the mornings across the misty fields. They would talk about the shooting and hunting they planned to do. Charles would put his arm around his young son's shoulders as they walked while Harry would excitedly ask questions about the hunt to come. Harry started going grouse hunting with his dad at age nine and soon became a good shot.

School Days

Harry attended all the same schools as William, following in his brother's footsteps in September 1987 at Mrs. Mynors's Nursery School in west London. The three-year-old was not very happy about going to school—perhaps because by that time, William had already moved on to the Wetherby School. On his first day of school, Harry cried and clung to his mother all through the ten-minute ride from Kensington Palace to the school. Once inside the school, he became very quiet and reserved, and cried when his parents left. "I had a lump in my throat when we left Harry,"[16] Charles recalls. Harry was shy by nature when he was very young, and at Mrs. Mynors's he refused to play games with the other children. He tended to hide in the playground instead. He would

Diana accompanies Harry, center, and William to Wetherby on the first day of school in 1989.

not speak in class nor fight back if someone pushed him. After a few weeks, however, he began to settle in at the school and start playing with the other kids.

After his initial adjustment, Harry's years at Mrs. Mynors's were happy. He appeared in the school's Nativity play as a shepherd. He also showed some natural leadership abilities, often taking charge in a game of follow the leader. One of his favorite activities at the school was painting. He loved being allowed to express himself freely with paint and crayons and frequently got paint splattered all over his clothes.

When Harry was five, he at last got to attend the same school as William. In September 1989, he joined his brother at the pre-preparatory Wetherby School, a school for boys up to about age eight. Harry was very bright and had a keen thirst for knowledge. One member of Prince Charles's staff described young Harry as "a walking encyclopedia—he positively loved learning new things, any scrap of information interested him as long as it was something new."[17]

At Wetherby, one of Harry's favorite classes was art. He especially liked painting and model making. His other favorite class was English. He also loved to write stories, and his teachers at Wetherby considered him to be a gifted writer. But his all-time favorite thing at Wetherby was anything that had to do with performing, including acting in plays and singing in the choir. At age six he already had good memorization skills and often took the lead in school plays, including *The Lion, the Witch, and the Wardrobe*.

A New Interest

By the time Harry was five, he was showing an interest in everything that had to do with the military. By that age, he had outgrown stuffed animals and loved to play with his toy soldiers and tank. He also had a replica uniform from the Parachute Regiment that was specially made for him, which he loved to wear when he played soldier.

Also when Harry was five, he watched a movie that had a profound effect on the rest of his life. Called *Zulu*, this 1964 film depicts the real-life Battle of Rorke's Drift in South Africa in 1879, in which a small band of British soldiers defeated thousands of Zulu warriors. Harry was fascinated by the movie. He showered

Harry takes a ride in a tank on a visit to a military base in Germany in 1993. His interest in the military began when he was a very young boy.

his father with questions about the battle. He was thrilled when his father promised to take him one day to visit the home base of the regiment involved at Rorke's Drift, the South Wales Borderers.

Harry also liked to question his family members about their experience in the military. Charles is colonel-in-chief of twelve regiments, and Harry was fascinated by his dad's various dress uniforms. Ken Wharfe recalls that Harry seemed obsessed by soldiers and the army. According to Wharfe, "Every birthday or Christmas, whenever Harry was asked what he wanted for his main present, his response was always the same: 'An army uniform—I really need a camouflage jacket.'"[18]

In 1993, when Harry was nine, he was thrilled when Diana took him to visit a military base in Germany. During a visit to the barracks of the Light Dragoons in Hanover, Harry got to wear a replica uniform and ride in a tank. He was photographed in a tank, a content smile on his young face. Around this same time, Diana also took him to a professional auto-racing track in England, where racing legend Jackie Stewart escorted Harry around the racetrack. For a brief time after that, Harry wanted to be a Formula One race car driver. But it was only a passing phase; Harry's heart was and always would be with the military.

Chapter 2

A Shattered Childhood

The once shy Harry came out of his shell early in his childhood and began to show a bold and fun-loving personality. Even though he was an impetuous child whose behavior at times could be rash and potentially dangerous, he was still a sweet, well-mannered, thoughtful boy who did well in school. Several events in his late childhood had a profound effect on young Harry, however, and as a teen and young adult his rebellious behavior sometimes spiraled out of control.

"Harry on a Mission"

From the time he was a little boy, Harry showed a boisterous and fearless side. Sometimes it was just innocent little-boy fun that got out of control. For example, one of his favorite games was to run into a field on the farm and chase cows. On one occasion, a cow Harry was chasing headed straight for his mother. Diana panicked and jumped over a fence to get out of the way, much to Harry's amusement. Another favorite activity was setting up a roadblock with his brother on the estate at Highgrove and requiring staff and police guards to pay a toll in order to pass. Harry sometimes took this game too far and threw stones at anyone who did not have the fee, until William stepped in to stop him. Behavior such as this once prompted Diana's brother, Earl Spencer, to refer to Harry as a "mischievous imp."[19]

Harry makes a silly face during an appearance on the balcony of Buckingham Palace with his mother, brother, and other members of the royal family in 1988. The prince has been known for being mischievous and adventuresome since he was a small child.

At other times his behavior was downright embarrassing, like the habit he developed in boyhood of dropping his pants and baring his backside. This may have been cute when he was younger and confined his moonings to private gatherings, but the thought that one day their son—who was often in the public eye—might drop his pants in public had his parents worried. It

A Royal Rascal

Harry was obsessed with the military as a child and constantly nagged his bodyguards to show him their guns and let him use their radios. Ken Wharfe, a Scotland Yard officer assigned to protect Diana and her two sons, recalls of Harry's persistent begging that "he was a pain in the backside."[1]

One day, Wharfe finally gave in and agreed to something he would deeply regret: He allowed the seven-year-old Harry to take the radio to several points within the Kensington Palace compound. The palace was guarded twenty-four hours a day, and Harry had promised to check in with Wharfe via the radio, so Wharfe did not think there was any harm in letting Harry have some fun. All went well at first, but when it was time for Harry to check in at one of his designated spots, a police barrier, he did not show up. The officer at the barrier told Wharfe that Harry had not been seen.

Panicked, Wharfe was on the verge of organizing a police search party when Harry finally radioed in. When Wharfe asked where he was, Harry happily replied, "I am at Tower Records in High Street, Kensington."[2] Harry had slipped off the grounds of the palace and walked down the main road to the iconic record store to have a look around. A relieved Wharfe ordered the young prince to return immediately.

1. Quoted in Robert Jobson. *Harry's War*. London: John Blake, 2008, p. 54.
2. Quoted in Jobson. *Harry's War*, p. 55.

was just the sort of thing the tabloids liked to get hold of; Harry was a royal, and his wild behavior had the potential to embarrass the monarchy.

Other times, Harry's rash and reckless behavior was dangerous. Harry took his first pretend parachute jump at age two by launching himself off the kitchen table at Highgrove; he managed to smash his head against the table and needed stitches, which left a scar. The disregard for danger that Harry was already showing by age two did not lessen any as he got older; in fact, he only became more fearless as time went by. For example, he and William had go-karts they loved to ride around the grounds at Highgrove, sometimes going as fast as 30 miles per hour (48kph). After watching the nine-year-old Harry try to take a corner at that speed and nearly wipe out, Charles put an end to go-karting in the countryside.

Harry's love of anything to do with the military sometimes combined with his impulsive nature to produce near-disastrous results. One such incident occurred during a shoot on the queen's estate at Sandringham when Harry was eleven and rashly fired at a low-flying bird. The bullet whizzed past a helper's head, missing him by inches. Another time, at Windsor Castle, a twelve-year-old Harry was photographed firing a shotgun out of the sunroof of a moving car while standing in the passenger seat. Predictably, the pictures appeared in the tabloids the next day.

Like all members of the royal family, Harry was constantly accompanied by bodyguards whose job was to make sure the young prince did not get hurt. In Harry's case, this proved difficult because he was so unruly and hard to control. Harry "could be like a little Rottweiler when he didn't want to stop doing something,"[20] observed one of his bodyguards. Once, during a driving lesson in his father's Range Rover at Highgrove, a seven-year-old Harry began to protest loudly when the bodyguard told him it was time to put the car away. As the bodyguard started to park in front of a stone wall, Harry reached his foot over and stomped down on the accelerator. The car smacked the wall, but, miraculously, no one was hurt, and the car was unscathed. Because of numerous close calls like this, Harry's bodyguards could never let him get too far from them. "There was no safe distance with Harry," one of his bodyguards once commented. "The combined armies of NATO [North Atlantic Treaty Organization] don't have the destructive force of Harry on a mission to cause mischief."[21]

A Stunning Blow

To the outside world, young Harry and his brother seemed to live a charmed life, complete with all the privileges of a royal lifestyle, a glamorous and doting mother, and a charming father

Details of Charles and Diana's divorce was front-page news all over the world in the early 1990s. The intense and sometimes insensitive media coverage of the end of his parents' marriage was both distracting and confusing for Harry at the time.

who was destined for the throne. In truth, however, Harry's world was beginning to crumble around him. Tensions in his parents' marriage that had been building for a long time inevitably spilled over to affect the boys. Although Charles and Diana made a great effort not to fight in front of them, by early childhood both Harry and William had picked up on the fact that their parents did not always get along.

As time went on, their parents' constant bickering and fighting was impossible to conceal from the children. The discord had a profound effect on the boys, who turned to each other for comfort during these difficult times. The staff at Highgrove often found the two young boys huddled together on the stairs with their hands over their ears whenever Charles and Diana were in a heated argument.

When Harry was eight, he joined his brother at Ludgrove School, a boarding school for boys in the countryside near London. Although Harry was glad to be nearer to his brother,

"A Tormented Young Man"

Diana's public admission of an affair with James Hewitt led to a persistent rumor that Harry, who bears a slight resemblance to the red-haired Hewitt, was actually Hewitt's son. Although Diana and Hewitt—as well as Diana's bodyguard, Ken Wharfe—claim they did not meet until Harry was two years old, the legend persisted.

Of all the rumors about his family that swirled in the tabloids, those that questioned his paternity were the most disturbing to the young prince. "Harry has had to live with these stories that he is James Hewitt's son, which he most certainly is not," says British author Judy Wade. "He just happens to have red hair, just like all his cousins on the Spencer

James Hewitt, who had an affair with Diana, has been the subject of speculation about Harry's paternity.

side of the family. So, poor Harry is a tormented young man." Harry is fiercely loyal to his father, and any speculation that Charles may not be his biological father troubles him deeply. As a teen, Harry wanted to volunteer to take a DNA test and put an end to the rumors once and for all. However, the queen would not permit it; to allow a paternity test would be to admit that members of the royal family believed there was a possibility Harry may not be a Windsor.

Quoted in *Harry: The Mysterious Prince*. DVD. Directed by Alan Scales. London: BBC Worldwide/Infinity, 2005.

the two of them slept in separate dormitories, since they were different ages. At Ludgrove, Harry and William took comfort from the routine and sense of normalcy the school offered. They awoke at 7:15 each morning and washed up in a bathroom they shared with the other boys on their floor. After breakfast, Harry studied geography, history, science, and French. In the afternoons he swam in the pool or went to soccer practice at the playing fields. From six to eight every evening, all the boys were allowed to watch a few educational shows on TV.

The boys' sense of well-being at Ludgrove was soon shattered, however. In December 1992, just a few months after Harry started school there, Diana drove to Ludgrove to meet with the boys in private. She had some very difficult news for them: Their parents had agreed to formally separate. When they were told, William broke down in tears, but Harry responded by becoming very quiet, as was typical of him during times of extreme stress.

The news that Charles and Diana's fairy-tale marriage was coming to an end made headlines around the world. Rumors and nasty stories about their bitter separation and divorce were repeated in tabloids and on TV, including speculation that both had committed adultery. Media coverage only intensified when Charles admitted publicly that he had engaged in a long-term relationship with Camilla Parker-Bowles during his marriage. Diana, too, admitted she had carried on a five-year affair with a young cavalry officer named James Hewitt during her marriage. It seemed the media could not get enough of the salacious details of the failed royal marriage, and there was constant coverage of Harry's parents.

School officials at Ludgrove went to great lengths to shield Harry and William from the sensationalized stories about their parents. For example, staff members were told not to have their TVs on around students and not to leave newspapers lying about. Despite these efforts, Harry and William found out what was being said about their parents. William used to sneak into his bodyguard's room and turn on the TV or read the magazines and newspapers there. "I get this sick feeling in my stomach," William said, "every time I see my mother's picture or my father's picture in the newspapers. I know they're going to say something just terrible."[22] William, who had always been protective of Harry, took great pains to shield his younger brother from the nasty rumors swirling in the media, but even he could not stop Harry from hearing the stories of their parents' problems repeated by the other students.

When he first started at Ludgrove, Harry was a hardworking pupil who earned good grades. That began to change soon after his parents separated. By the time Harry was ten, he was having trouble concentrating in class. He lost interest in his studies, and his grades began to slip. He was often distracted by the incessant reports in the tabloids about his parents' separation, most of them untrue. This was a very confusing time for Harry, who was too young to truly understand what was going on. One teacher at Ludgrove recalled, "Harry just became more and more quiet."[23]

Both parents tried to distract the boys from the emotional turmoil surrounding their separation. For example, Diana took them to a go-kart track during a school break soon after Harry started at Ludgrove. There they zipped around the track at 50 miles per hour (80kph) in brand-new go-karts with their names painted on the front, with their mother cheering them on from the sidelines. But the reality of his parents' situation proved very difficult for young Harry to forget for long. The Christmas he was nine, the strain really started to get to him. He and William spent the holiday with their father at Sandringham, and Harry missed his mother profoundly. Two days after Christmas he went for a long, solitary walk around the estate; a worker who saw him reported that the young prince was "crying his eyes out."[24]

An Unspeakable Tragedy

When his parents' divorce was finalized in 1996, it was a terrible blow to Harry. But there were darker days still ahead. Within a year an unspeakable tragedy would mark the beginning of his teen years and change his life forever.

Harry's world was turned upside down on the last day of August 1997. He and William were vacationing at Balmoral Castle, their summer home in Scotland, with their father. They had not seen their mother for a month and were expecting her to fly home

From left, Prince Philip, William, Earl Spencer, Harry, and Prince Charles walk behind the casket during Princess Diana's funeral procession through the streets of London in 1997.

from France the next day. Harry, who was two weeks shy of his thirteenth birthday, missed Diana terribly and could not wait to see her. Instead, shortly after 7:00 A.M., Harry felt his brother gently shake him awake. A red-eyed William and Charles delivered him the worst news of his life. His mother had been seriously injured in a terrible car crash in Paris during the night. Although doctors tried for hours to save her, Diana was dead. Harry broke down in tears, and the three of them sat on his bed, hugging each other and sobbing uncontrollably.

In the days that followed, Harry was numb with shock. At a church service he attended with Charles and William shortly after hearing of his mother's passing, Harry whispered to his father, "Are you sure Mummy is dead?"[25] When viewing the mountains of flowers and cards that had been left by mourners outside Balmoral, Harry was overcome with grief and clung tightly to his father's hand as he knelt to read the cards. On the day before her funeral, when Charles took the boys to the chapel where their mother's body lay so they could have a final good-bye in private, a trembling Harry could not bring himself to look at her.

The next morning, Harry and William walked with Prince Charles, Prince Philip (Queen Elizabeth's husband), and Earl Spencer (Diana's brother) behind Diana's casket in a funeral procession through the streets of London. Her casket was draped with flowers. Nestled atop a wreath of white roses was a square white card on which Harry had written simply "Mummy." One of the 1.5 million mourners who lined the two-mile (3.2km) route recalled, "As the boys appeared, everybody who was near them averted their eyes. If you had thought about Diana's sons for six days, to look at them now was impossible. People stared at the road, waiting for the coffin to pass."[26]

The two grief-stricken boys remained stoic during the emotionally grueling march, which Earl Spencer referred to as "a tunnel of grief" and "the most harrowing experience of my life."[27] Neither boy cried, though Harry, fighting to keep the tears from spilling, kept his head down and his fists tightly clenched. During the funeral service in Westminster Abbey, however, Harry could no longer control his tears. Sitting beside his openly crying brother, Harry buried his face in his hands and wept.

Drawing Closer

Harry's normally upbeat, easygoing nature changed dramatically after Diana's death. He became withdrawn and was prone to dark moods and crying spells for several weeks afterward. He would sometimes break down without warning, and in the evenings he cried himself to sleep, cradled in his nanny's arms. His nanny, a young woman named Tiggy Legge-Bourke, played an important part in comforting the emotionally fragile young prince. More than anything else, though, it was Harry's close relationship with his father and brother that helped him cope with the loss of his mother.

Despite often being portrayed in the media as an aloof and emotionally distant father, Charles had always been very loving and affectionate with both his sons. In the aftermath of Diana's

From left, William, Charles, and Harry hit the slopes at Whistler Mountain Resort in British Columbia, Canada, in March 1998. Skiing trips and other vacations helped Diana's sons and their father heal and grow closer after her death.

death, his relationship with them grew even closer. In an effort to distract Harry from his terrible loss, Charles took him on a trip to Africa just two months after Diana's death. Harry enjoyed the time alone with his dad, as well as the change of pace from school. He got to go on a safari in Botswana, visit a Zulu village, and see the Spice Girls in concert in Johannesburg, South Africa, which was the highlight of the trip for the young fan. In addition to taking Harry to Africa, Charles also frequently took both boys skiing, which appealed to Harry's athletic, daredevil nature.

While Harry and William grew closer to their father, they also grew closer to each other. After Diana's death, William's protectiveness toward his younger brother increased. The fifteen-year-old William, mature beyond his years, worried about how Harry was coping with their loss, especially when the two of them had to return to school only a few days after Diana's funeral. Going back to school that fall was doubly difficult for Harry because he was still at Ludgrove, while William had already moved on to Eton

Headstrong Harry

Harry and William are very close, and William's behavior enormously influenced Harry's as a child. Still, they view the world very differently, and each goes about making decisions in his own way. Whereas William always looks at all sides of an issue before making a decision (because as future king he cannot afford to make blunders), Harry does not have the pressure of being king—and has a very different way of thinking. A member of Prince Charles's staff recalls:

> If [Harry] wants to do something he just goes straight ahead and does it without giving any consideration to the consequences. That's not to say he is a bad boy, he's not. Harry is one of the nicest people you could ever meet, there is nothing he wouldn't do for anyone. Harry's only problem is that he doesn't always think things out. If Harry wants to make a goal for football he'll knock two bits of wood in the ground as posts. ... The fact that the wood has just been pilfered from a royal bench doesn't really faze him.

Quoted in Mark Saunders. *Prince Harry: The Biography*. London: John Blake, 2002, p. 83.

College, a boarding school for young men. William called Harry every few days to check up on him.

Harry and William leaned on each other after Diana's death, just as they had during the strain of their parents' disintegrating marriage. "I am unbelievably proud of the two of them," Charles said. "They are really quite remarkable. I think they have handled a very difficult time with enormous courage and the gravest possible dignity."[28] As Harry has explained, he and William are fortunate because "we've got each other to talk to," and that fact is what has seen them through painful times. "We are both very grateful that, you know, each of us were there as a shoulder to cry on if we needed to,"[29] Harry said.

Harry at Eton College

A year after Diana's death, Harry joined William at Eton, where he wore the same uniform as everyone else: pinstriped pants, black vest and tail coat, wing collar, and white bow tie. Harry excelled at sports and became a top military cadet at Eton. Although he struggled somewhat academically, earning a D in geography, he enjoyed his art classes and participated in the school's drama department.

But while Harry was at Eton, he became embroiled in several scandals. William and Harry both engaged in underage drinking at Eton, something to which their bodyguards turned a blind eye. Always within 100 feet (30m) of the boys, even at school, the bodyguards were under orders not to stop the boys from experiencing a normal adolescence. A classmate of the princes recalls, "Their bodyguards just looked the other way while they threw up."[30] William was able to keep his antics private and avoid media scrutiny, but Harry was not so fortunate.

In the summer of 2001, when Harry was only sixteen years old, the paparazzi got photos of him drinking in a nightclub in Spain, and pictures of a drunken-looking Harry were published in the British tabloid *News of the World*. Then the story broke that Harry had not only drunk at a pub called the Rattlebone Inn near Highgrove but had smoked marijuana there, too. Prince Charles took Harry to talk to recovering drug addicts at a drug rehabilitation facility, Featherstone Lodge, in south London.

Controversy seemed to follow the young prince even after he graduated from Eton in 2003 and began his gap year—a year (or, in Harry's case, two years) taken off after completing school to travel and work abroad before entering the workforce, a university, or the military. In the fall of 2004, a former Eton art teacher claimed that Harry had cheated on his A-level art exam. A-level exams are similar to college entrance exams and are also used for admission to military academies—and Harry desperately wanted a career in the army. The teacher claimed that she had done much of the work for Harry on his art exam, an allegation that made headlines but was never proved.

Harry performs as Conrad in Eton's production of Shakespeare's Much Ado about Nothing *in 2003.*

Harry Out of Control

The accusation of cheating on his art exam was followed closely by two more scandals that threatened Harry's reputation as well as his prospects for entering a military academy. In October 2004, as Harry was leaving a London nightclub, he was met by the ever-present pack of paparazzi. A scuffle broke out, during which Harry screamed obscenities and was photographed taking a swing at a photographer. The next day, the photo was on the front page of a London tabloid, the *Evening Standard*.

It was not the first time Harry had blown his fuse in public; there were several instances of a teenaged Harry throwing temper tantrums and swearing on the polo field at the Beaufort Polo Club that were witnessed by reporters and sometimes caught in photos or videos. "He's got the ... Spencer fiery temper," says journalist Richard Kay. "He's on a short fuse, most of the time. And if he's provoked by the sight of photographers or the paparazzi hanging around, he can fly off the handle."[31] The media—and many members of the public—wondered whether the young prince had gone completely out of control.

No incident concerning Prince Harry's behavior raised more eyebrows, however, than one that took place at a costume party in January 2005 at the home of Richard Meade, a family friend. Harry wore the uniform of the German Africa Corps, a Nazi division that had fought in North Africa against the British in World War II. The tan uniform, complete with the swastika armband, was actually a costume, which Harry had rented from a costume shop for the party. Just as with the incident with the photographer outside the nightclub the previous fall, a photograph of Harry in the uniform appeared on the front page of a tabloid the following day, along with the blazing headline "Harry the Nazi."

The reaction was one of widespread shock and horror. The grandson of the queen of England, himself third in line to the British throne, appeared to be making light of the Nazis and the Holocaust, in which 6 million Jews perished in Nazi death camps. Harry was publicly condemned for his thoughtlessness,

A British tabloid makes front-page news of Harry's controversial Nazi costume in 2005. In response to criticism from around the world, Harry issued an official apology.

with one of the most scathing rebukes coming from the Simon Wiesenthal Center, an international Jewish human rights group. "This was a shameful act, displaying insensitivity for the victims," read a statement from the organization. "Not just for those soldiers of his own country who gave their lives to defeat Nazism, but to the victims of the Holocaust who were the principal victims of the Nazis."[32]

Harry issued an official apology, which read in part: "I am very sorry if I caused any offense or embarrassment to anyone. It was a poor choice of costume and I apologize."[33] But the backlash continued. Journalist Richard Kay explains, "He simply didn't think. There is a thoughtlessness about many of his actions. He doesn't seem to appreciate yet that what he does actually matters. If it had been one of his friends who'd dressed up in a German uniform, it wouldn't have mattered at all. But it is because it's Prince Harry, it's because he's the third in line to the throne, he has to be responsible."[34]

Doubts About Harry

Harry's rebellious behavior, and the Nazi uniform in particular, had cast serious doubts about his judgment and suitability for the military, as well as for the throne. The media and many members of the public began to question whether the volatile prince had the self-discipline required for a career in the army. Meanwhile, Harry did his best to cope with portrayals of him as a spoiled, out-of-control party prince but admitted, "I'd love to let it wash over me, but I can't—I don't think anyone can. It is hard."[35]

Sir Richard Needham, a British politician who had spent time with the royal family, agreed with Harry. "What a monstrous life those two boys have to live," Needham commented. "Why can't they live their own lives? It's really, really awful. They are the only people in this country born into something from which they have absolutely no escape and in which they are hounded, absolutely hounded."[36]

As Harry's gap year stretched into its second year, Harry seemed to be floundering, uncertain of what to do now that he had finished his schooling. Those who knew him hoped that his entering the military would help him find a focus for his life and redirect his energies in a positive way.

Chapter 3

The Soldier Prince

After finishing school at Eton, Harry was still searching for a suitable career for the second son of a king-to-be. During his gap year Harry went to Argentina, where he spent several weeks working on a polo ranch that belonged to the Tomlinson family, who were friends of his father. Always an avid sportsman, Harry considered becoming a professional polo player, and in fact, he was already a fully qualified rugby coach. He eventually made up his mind, however, to follow his lifelong dream of joining the military. Unlike William, who started at the University of St. Andrews after his gap year, Harry decided to forgo a college education altogether and instead enrolled at the Royal Military Academy Sandhurst.

Officer Cadet Harry Wales

Many predicted the army would help the young prince shed his party image and settle down. "Sandhurst brings people down to size," said former army major Charles Heyman. "It's a big reality check and, the further up the pyramid you are, the bigger the shock. It will change him. I think he'll mature quite quickly after forty-four weeks at Sandhurst. They will not care that he's Prince Harry."[37]

Located in southern England, Sandhurst is an elite military academy. In order to win a spot in the academy, Harry had to pass a four-day assessment that featured fitness tasks and a military planning exercise. He entered Sandhurst in May 2005 along with 270 other recruits for forty-four weeks of training. His father

Harry, second from right, marches with his fellow army cadets from the elite Royal Military Academy Sandhurst in June 2005.

accompanied him to Sandhurst on his first day, giving the twenty-year-old Harry a playful punch on the arm before leaving him to start his military training. "I am really excited," Harry said. "I want to get on with it and do the best job I can do."[38] After Harry enrolled and picked up the keys to his small room, he was given a red name badge bearing the word *Wales* in big white letters; during his training Harry was referred to as Officer Cadet Wales.

Harry was treated just like any other cadet at Sandhurst. He received no preferential treatment or special privileges, nor did he expect or want any. The first five weeks of their training were the toughest. The cadets were confined to their barracks, with no visitors, no alcohol, and no outside passes allowed. They were kept isolated from the outside world as part of the academy's program to remold their way of thinking and turn them into soldiers.

Life at Sandhurst during training was very structured and disciplined—as well as tough. Like all the other cadets, Harry had to get up at dawn, make his bed with crisp hospital corners, and fold his blankets into a neat square. He had his hair cropped short

Harry Taken Hostage

Harry proved that he has what it takes to be a soldier while he was still a student at Eton College. One of Eton's best and bravest military cadets, at age seventeen he volunteered for a training exercise in which he was taken hostage by five other cadets dressed as enemy soldiers.

Harry was separated immediately from his companion on the evening of the exercise, dragged away, and thrown roughly into a Land Rover. The "enemy soldiers" took him to an isolated barn, where, with a hood over his head, he was interrogated for nine grueling hours. One of

Harry's military training at Eton included a training exercise during which he was held hostage for nine hours.

the participants in the exercise explains, "They moved him around to disorientate him, forced him to stand leaning on his finger tips against the wall and to kneel. And they shouted at him but he did exactly as he should. He said he was scared and injured to distract them and would only tell them his name, date and place of birth."[1] Despite being tired, humiliated, and at times near tears, Harry repeatedly answered their screamed demands for more information by replying politely, "I'm sorry sir, I cannot answer that question."[2] The exercise finally ended at 5:00 A.M. when the soldiers returned him to Eton and dumped him on the ground. Harry earned high praise from his superior officers for behaving exactly as he had been trained—as a true soldier.

1. Quoted in Robert Jobson. *Harry's War*. London: John Blake, 2008, p. 76.
2. Quoted in Mark Saunders. *Prince Harry: The Biography*. London: John Blake, 2002, p. 198.

and wore the same army-issue black boots and green overalls as the other cadets. Their days included tasks such as polishing boots, ironing uniforms, intensive drill sessions, and grueling physical exercises. They all went through basic drill, weapons training, and map readings. They spent time in classrooms, on the parade grounds, and outdoors for training. Harry and the other cadets also attended leadership training classes.

Harry lost weight, his feet blistered, and he was shouted at by sergeant majors—just like everyone else in training with him. He says he was treated "like a piece of dirt" while at Sandhurst, but that the experience changed him for the better and helped him grow up. "Nobody's really supposed to love it, it's Sandhurst,"[39] Harry joked.

Since childhood, Harry had wanted to be a paratrooper, but by the time he had finished his training, he decided he wanted to join an infantry regiment. In part this was because the training at Sandhurst leans toward infantry training, but there was another reason for Harry's change of heart. "I do enjoy running down a ditch full of mud, firing bullets," he confessed. "It's the way I am. I love it."[40] Harry completed his training at Sandhurst in April 2006 and was commissioned as a second lieutenant in the Blues and Royals of the Household Cavalry Regiment, part of the British Army.

Harry the Bullet Magnet

Harry had always wanted to be taken seriously as a soldier, and he wanted to serve in active duty. He had formed close bonds with the dozens of men he commanded in his troop and wanted to be with them to lead them if they went into combat. "There's no way I'm going to put myself through Sandhurst and then sit on my arse back home while my boys are out fighting for their country,"[41] Harry said in 2005.

In February 2007 Harry got his wish. The Ministry of Defense announced that Harry would accompany his regiment to Iraq, where the United Kingdom had had troops stationed since 2003. He would serve as a troop commander and be in charge of several light tank reconnaissance vehicles. His deployment to Iraq would make Harry the first member of the royal family to be sent to a war zone since 1982, when his uncle, Prince Andrew, was sent to the Falkland Islands as a Royal Navy helicopter pilot during the brief war there. Concerns for Harry's safety were immediately raised; Britain's Ministry of Defense feared that, as a royal and a blood relative of the queen, he would be a target for kidnapping or assassination by terrorists. Furthermore, his very presence in a war zone would place those serving with him in extra danger.

These concerns were very serious, indeed. Soon after the announcement of Harry's deployment—which was widely reported in newspapers—Abu Zaid, the commander of an enemy insurgent brigade in Iraq, released a chilling statement. "We are awaiting the arrival of the young, handsome, spoiled prince with bated breath," Zaid said. "He will return to his grandmother but without ears."[42] The leader of another insurgent group made it clear that Harry would not be able to hide his identity in Iraq. The army and the Ministry of Defense realized it was very likely Harry would be specifically targeted if he were to go to Iraq. The situation led the media to nickname Harry "the bullet magnet."[43]

Given these issues, in May 2007 the army announced that Harry's deployment to Iraq had been canceled, due to concerns for his safety and that of his men. "There have been a number of specific threats—some reported and some not reported—which relate directly to Prince Harry as an individual," said General Richard Dannatt, the head of the British Army. "These threats expose not only him but also those around him to a degree of risk that I now deem unacceptable."[44]

It was a crushing blow for Harry, who was devastated to see his men off without being allowed to go to Iraq with them. Although he understood the army's decision, it was a difficult one for him to accept. He considered leaving the army altogether but eventually accepted the decision and decided to stay. "I would never want to put someone else's life in danger when they have to sit next to the bullet magnet,"[45] Harry explained. An official statement released on his behalf read: "He fully understands and accepts General Dannatt's difficult decision and remains committed to his Army career. Prince Harry's thoughts are with his troop and the rest of the battle group in Iraq."[46]

Harry appears in camouflage while on a training exercise in Cyprus April 2006. As a member of the army, Harry was eager to serve his country in combat operations in Iraq, but his deployment was cancelled because of security concerns.

Widow Six Seven

Although Harry accepted the army's decision not to deploy him to Iraq, he did not give up his efforts to serve as a frontline soldier. In June 2007 he met with senior officials in the Ministry of Defense, including Dannatt, to discuss a tour of duty in Afghanistan, where the United Kingdom had stationed troops since 2001. During the meeting, Harry emphasized that he was determined to serve in combat and stated that he would seriously consider leaving the military if he were not allowed to go. Top military officials did not want that to happen, so they came up with a plan for Harry to serve as a battlefield air controller in Afghanistan.

During the military's deliberations over sending Harry to Iraq earlier in the year, the media had published detailed reports about Harry's deployment, which probably contributed to the security breaches. This time, the military did things differently. Dannatt met off the record with newspaper and broadcasting executives and explained that in order for a tour of duty in a war zone to be successful for Harry, the media would have to agree to a voluntary news blackout. The British media executives agreed not to report anything about Harry's deployment, although they could not be responsible for foreign media or the Internet. Still, it was a key factor in being able to get Harry covertly into Afghanistan without inviting the same threats that he would be kidnapped or killed by insurgents.

In mid-December 2007, under the utmost secrecy, the twenty-three-year-old Harry flew to Helmand Province in southern Afghanistan. In an interview that was not made public until after his deployment ended, Harry said, "No one really knows where I am, and I prefer to keep it that way, for the meantime, until I get back in one piece. Then I can tell them where I was."[47]

He was elated to be joining his brothers-in-arms in the Household Cavalry Regiment and do his part in the war on terror. Conditions for those serving in Helmand were very austere. Nighttime temperatures plunged to well below freezing, the sleeping areas had no heat, and there was almost no running water and very little shelter. Those stationed there, including Harry, could not bathe, shave, or launder their uniforms for days at a time.

Harry sits on the side of his bunk surrounded by his gear at a military base in Afghanistan, where he was secretly deployed in December 2007. During his time in Afghanistan, he was given no special privileges, which was his preference.

The young prince got and expected no special privileges. For example, Christmas fell a few days after his arrival, and Harry received the same extra ten minutes on his army satellite phone that every other British soldier got for the holiday. Said David Baxter, a corporal who served in Helmand with Harry, "We were initially surprised to see him … but at the end of the day he is just treated the same as any other officer."[48] While in Helmand, Second Lieutenant Harry Wales ate army rations and slept on a cot or in a hole dug in the ground just like everyone else. He was proud to be just one of the men.

Being just like any other soldier extended to other areas of his tour of duty as well. Just as there had been concerns over his personal safety if he went into combat, there were concerns about him going out on patrol because of the risk he might be recognized by a local insurgent. However, in his camouflage uniform, the third in line to the British throne looked pretty much like all

Harry patrols a town in the Helmand Province during his stint in Afghanistan in late 2007 and early 2008. The British media agreed not to report on Harry's deployment as a security measure.

the other soldiers. As Harry put it, "Just walking around, some of the locals or the ANP [Afghan National Police]—they haven't got a clue who I am, they wouldn't know."[49]

Harry, who has been recognized almost everywhere he has ever gone from the time he was a baby, found such anonymity a welcome change of pace. "It's fantastic," he said. "I'm still a little bit conscious [not to] show my face too much in and around the area. Luckily, there's no civilians around here. ... It's sort of a little no-man's-land."[50] He was careful, however, to keep his face slightly covered whenever he was in more populated areas so that he would not risk being recognized and putting himself and his fellow soldiers in danger.

Harry's anonymity even extended to some of the other soldiers serving there. His duties in Helmand included firing a machine gun to repel an enemy attack, patrolling in hostile areas, and calling in air strikes against enemy targets. The pilots he spoke with for hours on the radio every day knew him only by his call name, Widow Six Seven. According to Baxter, "He has always got a rapport with the pilots. I'm sure they would be quite shocked as well if they knew who they were talking to."[51]

An End to the Blackout

The voluntary news blackout lasted longer than anyone had thought possible. Harry served in Afghanistan for ten weeks before the news of his whereabouts was made public. The information was first published on the website of an obscure Australian magazine and received very little notice around the world—until an American website, the Drudge Report, picked up the piece and ran it. Once word of Harry's whereabouts appeared on the influential political website, the word was out for good, and the British news media began to report the news as well.

Now that his cover was blown, Harry was made a prime target for the enemy. So he was pulled out of Afghanistan in February 2008 for his own safety and that of the men serving with him. This was the second blow Harry experienced to his army career, and he was disappointed and frustrated when his tour had to be cut short. Yet he was grateful for the time he had

"Those Are the Heroes"

After the news broke that he was in Afghanistan, Harry was forced to return to England. He was accompanied on the flight home by several wounded soldiers, two of whom were so seriously injured that they were unconscious during the entire flight. Meeting these wounded servicemen moved him and left a lasting impression on him, as he explains:

> Those are the heroes. Those were guys who had been blown up by a mine that they had no idea about, serving their country, doing a normal patrol. The bravery of the guys out there was humbling. I wouldn't say I'm a hero. I'm no more a hero than anyone else. If you think about it there are thousands and thousands of troops out there. ... The bravery of the guys out there is just humbling, it's amazing. There were a lot of people in a worse situation than me, that's for sure.

Quoted in Robert Jobson. *Harry's War*. London: John Blake, 2008, pp. 219–220.

spent there and said he wanted to return to the front lines "very, very soon."[52] Harry, who was promoted to lieutenant in April 2008, was awarded an Operational Service Medal for his service in Afghanistan.

More Military Training

After returning from Afghanistan, Harry continued his military training in the hopes of being able to return to combat soon. In 2009 he realized another lifelong dream when he began training to become an Army Air Corps helicopter pilot. As a pilot, his contact with people on the ground would be more limited than during his ten-week Afghanistan tour, and he would therefore be less likely to be recognized.

Harry poses in front of an Apache helicopter in 2011 during his flight training with the Army Air Corps.

Harry spent eighteen months learning to fly the Apache attack helicopter. British forces in Afghanistan used the Apache helicopter to gather intelligence, track enemy fighters, and provide cover for larger Chinook helicopters that transport supplies and troops. "It is a huge honour to have the chance to train on the Apache, which is an awesome helicopter,"[53] said Harry. As a major part of his training, he spent two months in the United States on an exercise known as Exercise Crimson Eagle. During this training in Arizona and California, Harry became proficient at handling the helicopter in mountain and desert conditions during both day and night. He also practiced firing the helicopter's weapons during various combat scenarios.

Harry, who holds honorary military appointments in both the Royal Navy and the Royal Air Force, was promoted to captain in April 2011. When he finished his Apache helicopter training in February 2012, Captain Wales was honored for his copilot skills with an award for best copilot gunner.

Early in 2012 it looked as though Harry's wish to return to the front lines would be granted. In February it was announced that he was scheduled to go back to Afghanistan as a helicopter pilot by the end of the year. He was again deployed to Helmand Province in early September to begin a four-month assignment as an Apache pilot. This time around, there was no media blackout, because as a helicopter pilot he would be less vulnerable to attacks than when he was on foot patrols five years earlier. Harry's military career has earned him the respect and admiration of people around the world.

Chapter 4

Philanthropy and Royal Duties

In addition to his military career, Harry's charitable activities and his dedication to his royal duties have helped changed the public's image of him from a wild child to a supportive and caring young man. He has shown himself to be a true humanitarian, much like his mother.

Keeping a Legacy Alive

Harry has made it clear he intends to carry on Diana's legacy of helping others less fortunate. His mother was well known for her humanitarian efforts, including her work to help the underprivileged, the poor, and the sick, particularly those afflicted with HIV/AIDS. She related to people in a way that no member of British royalty had ever done before. She was photographed hugging AIDS patients, for example, which helped alleviate formerly widespread fears of being near AIDS sufferers as well as remove some of the social stigma of AIDS. She involved both her boys in her humanitarian efforts from the time they were little. For example, in 1993 Diana took both boys to a homeless shelter. Harry was shown card tricks by one man and played a game of poker with him. Diana wanted to make sure her sons knew about the harsh realities of life outside the palace walls.

Along with Charles, Diana often discussed the plight of the needy with Harry and William in family discussions after

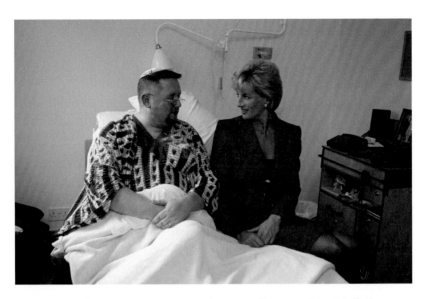

Diana, right, visits with a patient at the London Lighthouse, a center for people with HIV/AIDS, in 1996. Diana's extensive humanitarian work set an example that her sons have eagerly followed with their own charity projects.

dinner. She wanted them to grow up understanding that not everyone in the world shared their wealth and privilege, and as a result both boys understood there were others in the world who were disadvantaged. From the time they were young, Harry's and William's teachers noted their good manners and their consideration for others, traits Diana worked hard to instill in them.

Due in large part to his mother's efforts, Harry showed an early commitment to philanthropy. When he was eight he overheard his mother talking with members of the British Red Cross about the difficulties faced by people in Sarajevo, which was war-torn at that time. He immediately volunteered to go with an aid convoy that was headed to the former Yugoslavia. Much to the young prince's disappointment, both his mother and his father said it was too dangerous and that he was too young to go.

Diana still serves as a role model to Harry today. "I always think of my mother in everything I do," he says. "I hope she would be

Harry and William Lend a Hand

In December 2004 a major earthquake struck off the coast of the Indonesian island of Sumatra. It sparked a series of devastating tsunamis throughout the Indian Ocean. The tsunamis generated powerful waves that were up to 98 feet (30m) high. These waves crashed into coastal areas all

William, left, and Harry pack boxes of relief supplies for tsunami victims at a Red Cross center in 2005.

around the Indian Ocean, and more than 230,000 people in fourteen countries perished in what was one of the deadliest natural disasters in history. There was an outpouring of international aid and support for the survivors, which included 10 million people who were homeless or displaced.

After seeing reports of children who were orphaned by the disaster, both Harry and William were moved to tears. They volunteered to work in a warehouse and specifically asked to do something that required manual labor. "We just wanted to be hands on," said Harry. "We didn't want to sit back." The princes helped prepare and load hygiene packs, which contain essential toiletries like soap, toothbrushes, and toothpaste. The packs were sent by the Red Cross to the island nation of Maldives, where more than twenty thousand people were displaced or temporarily relocated due to the tsunami.

Quoted in BBC. "Princes Help Prepare Tsunami Aid." January 7, 2005. http://news.bbc.co.uk/2/hi/uk_news/4154687.stm.

proud of my work."[54] Harry first began venturing into his own charity work during his gap year, which began after he finished his studies at Eton College in 2003.

Forget Me Not

During William's gap year, he had worked on dairy farms, traveled to several countries, and spent ten weeks working with children in Chile. Harry was eager to do something similar. In addition to the weeks he spent in Argentina, Harry spent parts of his gap year in Australia, where he worked as a jackeroo (a trainee on a sheep or cattle ranch) for several months in the Australian outback. There he rounded up livestock, branded animals, and built fences. Harry also spent two months of the year in Lesotho, an impoverished nation in southern Africa. There the nineteen-year-old Harry spent time with orphans who had lost their parents to AIDS.

In Australia Harry was besieged by paparazzi and had to issue a public appeal for the media to leave him alone so he could learn about the country and life in the outback. But in Lesotho it was a different story; he welcomed the media attention that his presence brought to the plight of the orphans. He hoped his visit would

Harry plants a tree with a young orphan at a children's home in Lesotho in March 2004. His experiences in Lesotho inspired him to create a charity to help children who have lost their parents to AIDS.

help raise awareness and funds for them. He was photographed and filmed helping build a wire-mesh fence around the orphanage, playing with the orphans, and cradling tiny children in his arms. Harry's natural affinity with children was evident as he spoke softly to them and walked hand-in-hand with them. Harry described his experience with the orphans in Lesotho in the following way:

> I love children. Even back home—I just love children, but coming out here is different. I mean, you come out here and you see children everywhere. It's just hundreds of children. Up in the hills here, there's eight-year-olds, ten-year-olds looking after cattle, and their only means of protection is rocks. The nicest thing out here is, they don't know who I am. I'm just a normal guy to them, which is really, really nice, something that's so special, to be one of them. ... You should see their faces. I've got my video camera, I've filmed loads, I've taken loads of photographs—and they're all so happy.[55]

Harry was so moved by the AIDS orphans he met that he produced *The Forgotten Kingdom: Prince Harry in Lesotho*. The thirty-five-minute documentary shows footage of Harry interacting with children in a remote orphanage and talking to people in the village who have HIV or AIDS. "We want to do more, and we can,"[56] he says in the documentary. Harry also joined with Prince Seeiso of Lesotho in 2006 to found the charity Sentebale (which means "forget me not"). Founded in memory of their mothers, who both worked with AIDS patients and orphans, the charity helps vulnerable children in Lesotho—in particular, those who have lost their parents to AIDS. "I really feel that by doing this I can follow in my mother's footsteps and keep her legacy alive,"[57] Harry explains. As part of his work with Sentebale, Harry has traveled to Lesotho several times since his first visit, helping build orphanages, a school for the blind, and a refuge for young mothers. "Harry wants to make a difference," William explains, "and I've seen it with Sentebale. ... Out here, he is the star, to be honest. They love him out here, for what Sentebale has become."[58] Today, everywhere Harry travels, he participates in activities to help raise funds for Sentebale, such as charity rallies and polo matches.

The Princes' Charities

Harry and his brother grew up with an understanding that it was important for them to use their position in order to help others who are less fortunate than themselves. Like the rest of the royal family, Harry is a patron or president of many charities and organizations throughout the world. (A patron devotes large amounts of time, as well as uses his or her social status, to help raise awareness and funds for a charity.) He and William created the Princes' Charities Forum in April 2006 to help foster collaboration among their many charitable interests. The forum began with the princes' earlier patronages—Centrepoint, the Football Association, Tusk Trust, and Sentebale—and has grown to encompass about twenty organizations. Included in these are Dolen Cymru, MapAction, WellChild, the Khumbu Challenge 2009, and the Henry van Straubenzee Memorial Fund.

Because both Harry and William are in the military, efforts to support other soldiers are especially close to their hearts.

London's St. Paul's Cathedral is aglow in May 2008 during City Salute, an event sponsored by William and Harry to pay tribute to members of the British military and their families.

In May 2008 the two princes were instrumental as joint patrons in organizing City Salute, which paid tribute to the British Armed Forces with a major event outside St. Paul's Cathedral in London. The event kicked off with three Eurofighter Typhoon jets flying overhead and included a sound and light show. It also featured a parade with armored vehicles and ceremonial troops. City Salute was also a way to raise funds for Headley Court military hospital and the Soldiers, Sailors, Airmen and Families Association in order to support wounded soldiers and their families.

In September 2009 Harry and William launched the Foundation of Prince William and Prince Harry to further their humanitarian efforts. One of the main areas of focus for the foundation is young people who need guidance and support. The foundation is also involved in promoting sustainable development and conserving resources and the environment. A third focus is the welfare of those who serve or have served in the armed forces, especially those who have been wounded during their service. "We are both massively excited at the prospect of being able to help in whatever way we can, where we can," Harry said. "If we can use our position to do this, we are ready to."[59]

Walking with the Wounded

In March 2011 Harry further showed his support for his fellow servicemen and servicewomen when he took part in an event called Walking with the Wounded. This charitable expedition to the North Pole was held as a fund-raiser for injured military personnel to help with their rehabilitation. Harry served as royal patron for the expedition and also joined in part of the expedition, which included seriously injured veterans. Harry was very proud when Walking with the Wounded grew from being a single expedition into a full-fledged charity. At a press conference, he said that the charity "now blazes the trail in showing wounded servicemen and women that hope remains."[60]

In 2012 Walking with the Wounded began plans for five injured servicemen to climb the world's highest peak, Mount Everest in the Himalayas. Harry noted, "The expedition to the Himalayas, of which I am so proud to be patron, is raising money to train and

Harry, center, joins military servicemen in showing off their legs to promote Walking with the Wounded, a fund-raising expedition to the North Pole undertaken by a group of injured soldiers. Harry joined the group for part of their trek in March 2011.

educate those with ... injuries suffered in war to manage their transition into civilian employment." He said of those going on such expeditions for the charity, "Their courage defies words."[61]

His Royal Highness

In addition to serving as a trusted confidant and adviser, there are numerous ways in which Harry serves as a support to his father and brother. These include making public appearances and attend-

A Monarch's Duty

The king or queen of England is the constitutional monarch of sixteen sovereign states known as the Commonwealth realms, including the United Kingdom, Canada, Australia, and New Zealand, as well as the head of fifty-four nations that make up the Commonwealth of Nations. In addition, the British monarch is the head of the Church of England and appoints bishops and archbishops. The king or queen of England holds very little political power—with one notable exception. The monarch is the head of all of Britain's armed forces and is the only person in the nation with the power to declare war.

The monarch carries out many important tasks on behalf of the nation. These include making official visits abroad, as well as welcoming other world leaders who visit the United Kingdom. Even when not abroad, the monarch still spends a great deal of time traveling, visiting schools, hospitals, factories, and various organizations. Whether traveling or at home, the monarch carries out daily government duties that include reading and signing documents and reports from government officials. Handling the responsibilities of the British monarchy is a full-time job, one that dictates how the king or queen spends each day of his or her reign—and also a lifetime job that can only be "quit" by abdication or death.

Harry delivers a speech in Nassau, Bahamas, in March 2012 during a tour to mark Queen Elizabeth II's Diamond Jubilee. The tour marked Harry's first royal duties on behalf of the queen.

ing photo shoots and interviews. When Harry turned twenty-one in 2005, he joined his grandfather, father, and brother, as well as his uncle, Prince Andrew, as a counsellor of state, which means that he is able to stand in for the queen during certain state functions, such as attending meetings or signing documents. He also began making official royal visits of his own.

Harry's first official royal visit on behalf of the queen took place in March 2012. He visited Belize, the Bahamas, and Jamaica as part of the queen's diamond jubilee celebrations, which commemorated the sixtieth anniversary of her coronation. These three countries are part of the Commonwealth of Nations (nations that have Queen Elizabeth as their monarch and head of state), and Harry's visit was part of the royal family's tour of these nations during the queen's diamond jubilee year. "Prince Harry is really bouncing about the visit," said Jamie Lowther-Pinkerton, Harry's private secretary, in a statement announcing the visit. "The Prince is hugely looking forward to representing The Queen and he will bring his own brand of enthusiasm and energy to every event."[62]

During his weeklong tour of the three countries, Harry kept busy with official activities that included meeting with government officials, visiting with schoolchildren, talking with military personnel, taking part in military exercises, and attending services to mark the jubilee. He also enjoyed some of the tourist destinations these countries offer, such as the Good Hope Great House, a former plantation house in the stunningly beautiful Jamaican hills. Harry was given a tour of the house, which is now a hotel, and its scenic gardens. He also visited Xunantunich, a Mayan archaeological site in Belize, where he climbed the ancient pyramid, viewed a Mayan dance, and attended a festival that included food, music, and arts and crafts. Especially close to Harry's heart was his visit to Bustamante Hospital for Children in Kingston, Jamaica, because he is passionate about helping sick children. He toured several wards and play areas at the hospital, then unveiled a plaque at the entrance in honor of the queen.

After his tour of Belize, the Bahamas, and Jamaica, Harry traveled to Brazil on behalf of the British government. Part of the purpose of his visit was to promote British culture and exports and to support the launch of the GREAT campaign, which fosters links between Britain and Brazil. To kick off the campaign, he traveled by cable car to a plateau at the base of

Rio de Janeiro's Sugarloaf Mountain, where he delivered his first speech in Brazil. He also visited the world-famous Cristo Redentor (Christ the Redeemer) statue above Rio de Janeiro to help kick off the campaign. During his three-day tour of Brazil, Harry also participated in several events to help promote the 2012 Olympic Games in London, including starting a mile run for children and young adults, coaching touch rugby, and playing a game of beach volleyball.

While in Brazil, Harry also engaged in activities that supported his own charitable activities and interests. He took part in the Sentebale Polo Cup in São Paolo, which aimed to raise money and awareness for the charity's activities to help orphans and vulnerable children in Lesotho. Harry played for the Sentebale team and also delivered a speech at a lunch after the match. After the polo cup, which marked the end of Harry's official visit, he made a private journey to the interior of Brazil in order to learn more about conservation and the natural world, a personal interest of his.

Through his many charitable efforts, Prince Harry has shown he is a caring and sensitive young man who is devoted to alleviating the suffering of others. He has also represented the royal family and the British monarchy with warmth and enthusiasm.

Chapter 5

A Prince's Life

In real life, Prince Harry is a fun-loving and caring young man with an easygoing nature and a good sense of humor. He enjoys playing sports and engaging in other physical activities. Harry remains close to his family and supported both his father and his brother when they each got married.

Thanks largely to his military service and his commitment to his royal duties and to humanitarian causes, Harry has grown into a confident, capable, and respected member of the royal family—yet one who still knows how to have a good time.

Everyday Harry

Harry is soft spoken, charming, and poised. "Both boys have the same magic that their mother had," says writer Peter Archer. "It's amazing how they are able to so easily connect with people. You'd never suspect all the pressures to which they are almost constantly subjected."[63] Journalist Penny Junor adds of Harry, "He is utterly charming and far more sensitive than he is ever given credit for."[64]

Harry is a multimillionaire in his own right, just like William and the other members of his family. Diana's mother, Frances Shand Kydd, left them roughly one-fourth of her $4 million estate when she died in 2004, and Diana left them roughly $10.5 million each. In addition, each has inherited millions in assets as members of the royal family. Like his brother, Harry's inheritance was held in trust until he turned twenty-five; since then he has been allowed to spend the income generated by his portion of the

Harry, an outstanding athlete, plays polo in Brazil in March 2012. When not tending to his official military or royal duties, he enjoys sports, going out with his friends, and traveling.

estate, which is approximately five hundred thousand dollars a year. When he turns thirty in 2014, he will have access to all of the money he has inherited. Although he is rich, Harry prefers to save and invest his money, rather than blowing it on pricey indulgences.

Today, when Harry is not traveling around the world for charity, military training, or tours of duty, he lives at Clarence House, a royal residence in London. This four-story home, built in the early 1800s, is his official residence, as well as that of his father and Camilla. It was also William's home until his marriage in 2011.

Just as when he was a child, Harry still likes to live his life as normally as possible—while still carrying out his royal duties. Although he is a member of a royal family and has grown up with privilege, Harry is a lot like any normal young man his age. As a young adult, he is very rugged and likes all kinds of sports. He also enjoys going dancing and can sometimes be found partying in nightclubs, wearing jeans and a collared shirt and surrounded by his royal bodyguards and the constant stream of young women who hope to catch his eye. Although he has left behind the wild days of his youth, he still enjoys a beer now and then. He also smokes cigarettes, a habit he continued even after entering the army.

Harry hates to be called "sir" or "Your Highness" and prefers just to be treated like a regular guy. This became evident when he was in the United States in the fall of 2011 for military training. During time off from his helicopter training, Harry made headlines by shopping at a Walmart store in California. There he filled his cart with ordinary items such as bananas, cola, frozen pizza, and beer. He ordered tacos from a nearby food stand, where he stood in line just like everybody else. Harry even visited an Irish pub in San Diego during his months in the United States and behaved like a true tourist when he obliged a young engaged couple in the pub by taking their picture. Harry further enjoyed some of the everyday sights of the American West by taking a motorcycle ride on a Harley Davidson from Scottsdale, Arizona, to Las Vegas, Nevada. Clad in a black motorcycle helmet, silver aviator sunglasses, a plaid shirt, and faded jeans, he looked just like anybody else on the open road.

Harry is still very athletic and enjoys all the same sports he did when he was younger. He also likes hunting and rides with the Beaufort Hunt, a fox-hunting group, as do his father and brother—although since 2005, when fox hunting became illegal in England, they no longer shoot on the hunts. Harry still out-performs his big brother in polo, skiing, and virtually every other sport. Harry and William are both very competitive and will try to best each other—even if they are on the same team. According to Richard Kay, a columnist for the British tabloid the *Daily Mail*, "[Harry is] a great sportsman, fearless skier, very brave on a polo pony, and again, on a horse chasing after foxes and hounds. He is actually better than William in most sports."[65]

Harry's Friends

Harry is a fun-loving young man with a good sense of humor and many friends. Soccer superstar David Beckham is one of his best friends. They are often seen paling around and hanging out in London nightclubs.

Harry is a very loyal friend who goes out of his way to help a friend in need. In late 2011 Harry came to the aid of his friend Thomas van Straubenzee, who was mugged while talking with the prince on his cell phone. Harry rushed across London to help his friend, but by the time he got there Van Straubenzee was gone. So Harry went to the local police station, where Van Straubenzee was reporting the crime, to support his friend and give a statement to police.

Thomas van Straubenzee is the older brother of one of Harry's closest friends at Ludgrove, Henry van Straubenzee. Henry was killed at age nineteen when the car in which he was riding crashed into a tree in 2002. Henry's death was devastating for Harry, who had lost his mother in a tragic car crash only five years earlier. Today, Harry, Thomas, and William are patrons of the Henry van Straubenzee Memorial Fund, which is dedicated to improving education for the children of Uganda.

Along with Harry's loyalty, however, comes a lot of publicity for anyone who is his friend. Harry admits that friends of his and William's get hounded by photographers, just as they do. "It's just as hard for our friends as it is for us," Harry says. "Our friends have to put up with a lot when it comes to us."[66] Adds William, "There's a lot of baggage that comes with us, trust me, a lot of baggage."[67]

Two Royal Weddings

In April 2005 Harry's father, Prince Charles, at long last married the woman he had loved for decades, Camilla Parker-Bowles. Harry and William learned as kids about the emotional anguish their father's affair with Camilla had caused their mother. By 2005, however, they both had met and gotten to know Camilla, and were openly supportive of their father's second marriage. Says a longtime friend of both princes, "William and Harry always wanted their father to be happy, and by this time they were so used to Camilla being there, they didn't feel that they were betraying their mother any longer."[68] They both served as witnesses at the wedding. After the ceremony, both the young princes kissed her on both cheeks. They also showed their support by decorating their father's car with Mylar balloons and being photographed with Camilla for the first time.

Harry and William are both very close to Camilla and love her very much. She has never tried to take the place of their own

Harry waves to onlookers from a carriage taking him and a few young attendants to Buckingham Palace after the wedding of Prince William and Kate Middleton, at which he served as best man, in April 2011.

mother but rather has become a beloved stepmother to them. Harry says he and William "love her to bits" and are grateful to her for being so wonderful to their father. "She's made our father very, very happy,"[69] he says.

In addition to gaining a stepmother, Harry gained a sister-in-law when William married longtime girlfriend Kate Middleton in 2011. Harry served as best man and also helped plan the wedding. He was delighted that William had proposed to Kate. "I've always wanted a sister and now I've got one,"[70] he says.

Harry and William Today

Harry's best friend has always been his big brother, and that remains true today. Despite their busy schedules, they still talk to each other almost every day. There is an easy rapport between the brothers that is part of their good-natured sibling rivalry. They often tease each other, jokingly put each other down, and laugh about it. For example, William sometimes affectionately calls Harry "Ginger," a reference to Harry's reddish hair—and Harry counters by teasing his brother about going bald.

During one interview, Harry joked that his older brother was so lazy that he was still crawling at age six. And when the interviewer used the word *dutiful* to describe William, Harry asked, "Was that 'dutiful' or 'beautiful'?" It was all in good fun, of course. The brothers are just as likely to compliment one another as they are to tease. For example, when pressed later in the same interview to describe his brother, Harry replied earnestly, "You know, he works very hard. He's definitely the more intelligent one of the two of us."[71]

Harry and William still seem to know what each other is thinking and still finish one another's sentences. They understand and support one another in everything each undertakes and through all of life's ups and downs. Harry feels like his brother is the one person he can talk to about anything. They have always shared a deep bond, and this has only increased since their mother's death. "He is the one person on this earth who I can actually really... we can talk about anything," Harry says. "We understand each other and we give each other support.

Harry, left, and William share a laugh while entangled by an African rock python during a visit to Botswana in 2010. The brothers are known to frequently joke with and tease each other, and as adults, they remain as close as they were as young boys.

If I find myself in really hard times, then at least I can turn to him, and vice versa."[72]

Prince Charming

Harry earned a reputation as a ladies' man while he was still a teen and has been linked romantically with a succession of young women over the years. The most prominent of these relationships was with the Zimbabwe-born Chelsy Davy, his first serious romance. They first met while she was a student at Cheltenham Ladies' College, near Highgrove House, Harry's family's country home. After graduating from Cheltenham, Davy attended the University of Cape Town in South Africa. It was there, in Cape Town, that the two fell in love when Harry stopped for a visit on his way to Lesotho during his gap year. A friend of Harry's reported that while sitting next to the fire

Chelsy Davy, left, was Harry's on-again, off-again girlfriend for six years until the couple broke up for good in 2010.

on a camping trip in Botswana, Harry "couldn't stop talking about her."[73] William told friends that Harry was "madly in love"[74] with Davy. Like Harry, Davy loves the outdoors and adores animals. She is also an attractive young woman, with blonde hair, tanned skin, and a bright smile. In an interview early in their relationship, Harry described her as "very special" and "amazing."[75]

Harry to the Rescue

While Harry was in the United States for military helicopter training in the fall of 2011, he made quite an impression on one young woman. One weekend in October, Harry and some friends were watching a rugby match on TV at the Andaz Hotel's rooftop pool in San Diego when he noticed that a young woman had been tossed fully clothed into the pool. Harry rushed to her aid, but by the time he got there she had already emerged from the water, soaking wet. He offered her his towel, wrapping it around her to keep her warm. Twenty-three-year-old Lindsay Swagerty, an office worker, was delighted to meet the prince and even more delighted by his gentlemanly gesture. She kept his towel as a souvenir, and the following night she and several of her friends met him and his friends for drinks. "He is probably the most charming man I'll ever meet," says Swagerty.

Quoted in Simon Perry and Stephen M. Silverman. "Prince Harry Comes to the Rescue at Pool Party." *People*, October 12, 2011. www.people.com/people/package/article/0,,20395222_20536242,00.html.

Although the two were very much in love, they broke up and got back together again several times over the course of their stormy relationship. Davy was present at many of the most significant events of Harry's life during this time, including his graduation from Sandhurst. There were persistent rumors that the two planned to marry, yet after six years of dating off and on, the couple called it quits in 2010.

Since his split with Davy, there have been several rumors concerning his love life. One of these was that he was involved with Pippa Middleton, the younger sister of William's wife. Harry and Pippa have met each other several times for tea since the royal wedding and have talked on the telephone on numerous occasions. Harry even ended his best man's speech at William and Kate's wedding by suggesting that Pippa should call him sometime. He was only joking around, though, and he and Pippa are only friends. Harry laughed off any suggestion that the two of them are anything more than friends. "Pippa? ... No," Harry told a reporter in June 2011. "I am not seeing anyone at the moment. I'm 100 per cent single."[76]

Harry has been linked romantically with many other women, including Florence Brudenell-Bruce, an English lingerie model. The two have many mutual friends and have known each other for several years. They dated briefly in 2011 before calling it quits, in part because Harry was focusing on his army career. Says Harry, "I'm working a lot at the moment, so dating and watching TV are the last things I have time for."[77]

Harry's Legacy

In 2007 the world got the opportunity to see a more mature Prince Harry. That summer marked the ten-year anniversary of Diana's death, and Harry and William decided to honor her memory with a concert and a church service. The two young princes worked together to plan and host the memorial concert, held on July 1, 2007, which would have been their mother's forty-sixth birthday. Held at Wembley Stadium in London, the concert was attended by more than sixty thousand people, with another 500 million in 140 countries around the world watching on TV.

Proceeds of ticket sales, estimated at $10 million, were divided among Diana's favorite charities, as well as Sentebale, which Harry had founded in her memory. The star-studded concert included performances by Rod Stewart, Duran Duran, and Kanye West, among many others, as well as a tribute by Andrew Lloyd Webber prepared especially for the occasion. Perhaps the most notable performance was that of Elton John, who was one of Diana's closest friends and had sung at her funeral.

Helping to organize and host the concert demonstrated that Harry was capable of handling the adult responsibilities that come along with his royal status and his place as third in line to the throne. This more mature side was demonstrated even further during the church service that was held in a London chapel on August 31 to mark the tenth anniversary of Diana's

Harry, left, and William take part in preparations for the Concert for Diana at London's Wembley Stadium in 2007. The princes planned and hosted the all-star event to mark what would have been their mother's forty-sixth birthday.

death, which Harry and William had organized with the help of Diana's siblings.

Prince William read a passage from the Bible, but moments later, it was Harry who delivered the tribute to their mother. Harry stepped proudly before the congregation of almost five hundred people—including Queen Elizabeth, Prince Philip, Prince Charles, and the new prime minister, Gordon Brown—and a global TV audience of millions. Tall, handsome, and dynamic, Harry spoke eloquently and with a mature poise that surprised many. In a speech he and his brother wrote together, Harry described their mother in the following words: "She was our guardian, friend and protector. She never once allowed her unfaltering love for us to go unspoken or undemonstrated. She will always be remembered for her amazing public work. But behind the media glare, to us, just two loving children, she was quite simply the best mother in the world."[78] The world saw that Harry had grown from the lost little boy walking with a bowed head behind Diana's casket into a confident and well-spoken young man. What was more, as he neared his twenty-third birthday, Harry was no longer standing in the shadow of his older brother.

Part of Harry's legacy is keeping Diana's legacy alive, through his charitable and humanitarian activities. Harry wants very much for people to remember all the good things his mother accomplished while she was alive, such as raising awareness of AIDS and speaking out against landmines. "I think people will always have a fascination about her,"[79] Harry says. He sees it as his duty to make sure that people remember her for the right reasons—and not for any of the sensationalized stories that continue to circulate about her. "It still upsets me now, the fact that

"A Constant Reminder"

In 2007 Harry was interviewed by Matt Lauer on the eve of the celebrations to honor Diana's forty-sixth birthday and the ten-year anniversary of her death. During the interview Harry spoke candidly about missing his mother and said that the ten years since her passing had gone by very slowly for him:

> Really, really slowly actually. It's weird because I think when she passed away there was never that time, there was never that sort of lull. There was never that sort of peace and quiet for any of us due to the fact that her face was always splattered on the paper the whole time. Over the last ten years I personally feel as though she has been, she's always there. She's always been a constant reminder to both of us and everybody else. And therefore I think when you're being reminded about it does take a lot longer and it's a lot slower.

Quoted in Matt Lauer. "In Honor of Diana." Transcript. MSNBC.com, June 27, 2007. www.msnbc.msn.com/id/19190534.

we didn't have much of a chance as children to sort of spend time with her," he once said. "But the time we did spend with her was amazing and as a mother, as anybody would say about their mother, [she was] just amazing."[80]

King Harry?

Harry has proved himself to be a responsible young man who is caring, sensitive, and outgoing. Even when he was a child, some who knew him wondered whether his bold yet easygoing personality might make him better suited to the role of monarch than his brother's more shy and reserved personality. This was something noted by his parents as well as others close to the family.

From time to time when they were growing up, William would have moments when he did not want the responsibility of being king. It was a heavy burden that sometimes prompted him to declare he would rather step aside and leave the throne to

Prince Charles, left, is next in line to the throne of England, followed by William, right, then Harry.

Harry instead. Whenever such outbursts occurred, Harry would respond that he would be happy to take William's place on the throne. "I'd love it!"[81] Harry would say.

It is not unheard of for a king to abdicate, or step aside—most famously in 1936, when King Edward VIII of England gave up the throne so he could marry twice-divorced Wallis Simpson, leaving his younger brother, George VI, to take his place as king. This is not only a part of history, but a part of Harry and William's family tree; had Edward not abdicated, Elizabeth would not have eventually become queen and her grandson William would not currently be second in line to the throne. But William long ago accepted his fate and is ready to embrace his role as king when the time comes. Still, Harry is sometimes asked during interviews if he worries about William abdicating and leaving him with the responsibility of being king. And Harry worries sometimes that William might just do it. "He assures me that he's not going to do that," Harry says, laughing nervously, but adds, "I've had dreams."[82]

Abdication aside, Harry could still become king one day, if both Charles and William were to die without William producing an heir. Since William and Kate's marriage in 2011, rumors have run rampant that they are expecting a baby; should they have a child, Harry would then drop down to fourth in line to the throne and it would become increasingly unlikely he would ever actually assume the throne.

The Future of Prince Harry

What is more likely for Harry is that he will continue to serve his country in both his capacity as an officer in the British Army and as a member of the royal family. He will also offer invaluable support to his father, and then his brother, when they each assume the throne. But more than that, Harry—along with William—has become a symbol of the monarchy in transition as it gradually evolves from centuries-old traditions and into the twenty-first century. Jennie Bond, a British journalist, writes, "Dear old Harry. Just hearing his name makes everyone smile because he's so mischievous and funny. He's helped make the monarchy cool in the eyes of young people, which is very important for its future."[83]

Indeed, Harry is a very modern royal. He and his brother will carry the monarchy from the old days into the future. As they uphold time-honored British traditions, they will simultaneously breathe new life into the royal family. And Harry, the royal maverick, will continue to do things in his own endearing way.

Notes

Introduction: The Maverick Prince

1. Quoted in ITN (Independent Television News). *The Forgotten Kingdom: Prince Harry in Lesotho*. Video. www.sentebale.org/home/PrinceHarryLesotho.html.
2. Quoted in *Harry: The Mysterious Prince*. DVD. Directed by Alan Scales. London: BBC Worldwide/Infinity, 2005.
3. Quoted in Sentebale. "Prince Harry's Story." www.sentebale .org/home/PrinceHarry.html.

Chapter 1: The Spare Heir

4. Quoted in Robert Jobson. *Harry's War*. London: John Blake, 2008, p. 23.
5. Quoted in Jobson. *Harry's War*, p. 26.
6. Quoted in Mark Saunders. *Prince Harry: The Biography*. London: John Blake, 2002, p. 18.
7. Quoted in Christopher Andersen. *Diana's Boys*. New York: William Morrow, 2001, p. 63.
8. Quoted in Jobson. *Harry's War*, p. 23.
9. Quoted in *Harry: The Mysterious Prince*.
10. Quoted in Jobson. *Harry's War*, p. 41.
11. Quoted in Saunders. *Prince Harry*, p. 44.
12. Quoted in Andersen. *Diana's Boys*, pp. 121–122.
13. Quoted in *Harry: The Mysterious Prince*.
14. Quoted in *Harry: The Mysterious Prince*.
15. Quoted in Jobson. *Harry's War*, p. 35.
16. Quoted in Ingrid Seward. *William and Harry*. New York: Arcade, 2003, p. 92.
17. Quoted in Saunders. *Prince Harry*, p. 83.
18. Quoted in Jobson. *Harry's War*, p. 53.

Chapter 2: A Shattered Childhood

19. Quoted in Andersen. *Diana's Boys*, p. 122.
20. Quoted in Jobson. *Harry's War*, p. 44.

21. Quoted in Saunders. *Prince Harry*, p. 58.
22. Quoted in Andersen. *Diana's Boys*, p. 117.
23. Quoted in Andersen. *Diana's Boys*, p. 113.
24. Quoted in Saunders. *Prince Harry*, p. 98.
25. Quoted in Andersen. *Diana's Boys*, p. 22.
26. Quoted in Andersen. *Diana's Boys*, p. 31.
27. Quoted in Christopher Andersen. *After Diana*. New York: Hyperion, 2007, p. 21.
28. Quoted in Saunders. *Prince Harry*, p. 133.
29. Quoted in Matt Lauer. "In Honor of Diana." Transcript. MSNBC.com, June 27, 2007. www.msnbc.msn.com/id/19190534.
30. Quoted in Andersen. *After Diana*, p. 100.
31. Quoted in *Harry: The Mysterious Prince*.
32. Quoted in Simon Jeffery. "Prince Harry Urged to Visit Auschwitz." *Guardian* (Manchester, UK), January 13, 2005. www.guardian.co.uk/uk/2005/jan/13/monarchy.simonjeffery.
33. Quoted in Jobson. *Harry's War*, p. 109.
34. Quoted in *Harry: The Mysterious Prince*.
35. Quoted in Andersen. *After Diana*, p. 209.
36. Quoted in Penny Junor. *The Firm*. New York: Thomas Dunne, 2005, p. 414.

Chapter 3: The Soldier Prince

37. Quoted in Jobson. *Harry's War*, p. 122.
38. Quoted in BBC. "Harry Begins Sandhurst Training." May 8, 2005. http://news.bbc.co.uk/2/hi/uk_news/4526077.stm.
39. Quoted in *Telegraph* (London). "I Was Treated like Dirt at Sandhurst. It Did Me Good." September 15, 2005. www.telegraph.co.uk/news/uknews/1498418/I-was-treated-like-dirt-at-Sandhurst.-It-did-me-good.html.
40. Quoted in *Telegraph* (London). "I Was Treated like Dirt at Sandhurst. It Did Me Good."
41. Quoted in Jobson. *Harry's War*, p. 121.
42. Quoted in Jobson. *Harry's War*, p. 139.
43. BBC. "Prince Harry on Afghan Front Line." February 28, 2008. http://news.bbc.co.uk/2/hi/7269743.stm.

44. Quoted in Matthew Moore. "Prince Harry Will Not Be Deployed to Iraq." *Telegraph* (London), May 16, 2007. www.telegraph.co.uk/news/uknews/1551688/Prince-Harry-will-not-be-deployed-to-Iraq.html.

45. Quoted in Jobson. *Harry's War*, p. 148.

46. Quoted in Thomas Harding and Caroline Davies. "Iraq Is Too Dangerous for Harry, Says Army." *Telegraph* (London), May 17, 2007. www.telegraph.co.uk/news/uknews/1551796/Iraq-is-too-dangerous-for-Harry-says-Army.html.

47. Quoted in *Telegraph* (London). "Prince Harry in Afghanistan: The Battlefield Air Controller." Video. February 28, 2008. www.telegraph.co.uk/news/uknews/prince-harry/8579275/Prince-Harry-in-Afghanistan-the-Battlefield-Air-Controller.html.

48. Quoted in *Telegraph* (London). "Prince Harry in Afghanistan."

49. Quoted in Jobson. *Harry's War*, p. xviii.

50. Quoted in Jobson. *Harry's War*, p. xix.

51. Quoted in *Telegraph* (London). "Prince Harry in Afghanistan."

52. Quoted in BBC. "Prince Harry Rejects 'Hero' Label." March 2, 2008. http://news.bbc.co.uk/2/hi/uk_news/7273129.stm.

53. Quoted in Rebecca English. "Air Corps Blimey! Chelsy Davy Looks Simply Stunning in Cream Babydoll Dress as Prince Harry Gets His Helicopter Wings." *Daily Mail* (London), May 7, 2010. www.dailymail.co.uk/tvshowbiz/article-1274439/Prince-Harry-train-Apache-attack-helicopter-pilot.html#ixzz1oRqmPM1q.

Chapter 4: Philanthropy and Royal Duties

54. Quoted in Gordon Rayner. "Prince Harry: I Think of My Mother in Everything I Do." *Telegraph* (London), December 17, 2010. www.telegraph.co.uk/news/uknews/theroyalfamily/8209168/Prince-Harry-I-think-of-my-mother-in-everything-I-do.html.

55. Quoted in ITN. *The Forgotten Kingdom.*

56. Quoted in ITN. *The Forgotten Kingdom.*

57. Quoted in Sentebale. "Prince Harry's Story."

58. Quoted in Sentebale. "Prince Harry's Story."
59. Quoted in Prince of Wales. "The Foundation of Prince William and Prince Harry." October 2, 2011. www.princeofwales.gov .uk/newsandgallery/focus/the_foundation_of_prince_ william_and_prince_harry_570302665.html.
60. Quoted in *Telegraph* (London). "Prince Harry: Proud to Be Named Walking with the Wounded Patron." Video. February 10, 2012. www.telegraph.co.uk/news/uknews/prince -harry/9074772/Prince-Harry-proud-to-be-named-Walking -with-the-Wounded-patron.html.
61. Quoted in *Telegraph* (London). "Prince Harry: Proud to Be Named Walking with the Wounded Patron."
62. Jamie Lowther-Pinkerton. "A Statement by Jamie Lowther-Pinkerton on Prince Harry's Overseas Tour to the Bahamas, Jamaica, Belize and Brazil." Prince of Wales, February 1, 2012. www.princeofwales.gov.uk/newsandgallery/focus/a_ statement_by_jamie_lowther_pinkerton_on_prince_harry_ s_ove_846689140.html.

Chapter 5: A Prince's Life

63. Quoted in Andersen. *After Diana*, p. 214.
64. Quoted in Junor. *The Firm*, p. 370.
65. Quoted in *Harry: The Mysterious Prince*.
66. Quoted in Lauer. "In Honor of Diana."
67. Quoted in Lauer. "In Honor of Diana."
68. Quoted in Andersen. *After Diana*, p. 227.
69. Quoted in *Telegraph* (London). "A Wicked Stepmother? No, We Love Her to Bits." September 15, 2005. www.telegraph .co.uk/news/uknews/1498421/A-wicked-stepmother-No-we- love-her-to-bits.html.
70. Quoted in BBC. "Royal Wedding: Prince Harry Hails 'Sister' Kate." December 17, 2010. www.bbc.co.uk/news/uk- 12022014.
71. Quoted in Lauer. "In Honor of Diana."
72. Quoted in Sally Pook. "I Don't Want to Change. I Am Who I Am." *Telegraph* (London), September 15, 2005. www .telegraph.co.uk/news/uknews/1498417/I-dont-want-to- change.-I-am-who-I-am.html.

73. Quoted in Andersen. *After Diana*, p. 210.
74. Quoted in Andersen. *After Diana*, p. 250.
75. Quoted in *Telegraph* (London). "Chelsy Is Very Special to Me—She's Amazing." September 15, 2005. www.telegraph .co.uk/news/uknews/1498419/Chelsy-is-very-special-to-me-shes-amazing.html.
76. Quoted in Katie Nicholl. "There's No Pippa Fling, Says '100 Per Cent Single' Prince Harry." *Daily Mail* (London), June 26, 2011. www.dailymail.co.uk/femail/article-2008197/Theres -Pippa-Middleton-fling-says-100-cent-single-Prince-Harry -Royal-family.html#ixzz1oMH3oGIA.
77. Quoted in Katie Nicholl. "There's No Pippa Fling, Says '100 Per Cent Single' Prince Harry."
78. Quoted in Jobson. *Harry's War*, p. 5.
79. Quoted in Lauer. "In Honor of Diana."
80. Quoted in Lauer. "In Honor of Diana."
81. Quoted in Andersen. *Diana's Boys*, p. 185.
82. Quoted in Andersen. *After Diana*, pp. 245–246.
83. Jennie Bond. "My Heroes and Heroines: Jennie Bond." *Telegraph* (London). February 14, 2012. www.telegraph .co.uk/news/uknews/the_queens_diamond_jubilee /9074093/My-Heroes-and-Heroines-Jennie-Bond.html.

Important Dates

1981

Harry's parents, Prince Charles and Lady Diana Spencer, marry at St. Paul's Cathedral in London, in a ceremony that is televised to 750 million people worldwide.

1982

Harry's older brother, Prince William Arthur Philip Louis, is born in London.

1984

Prince Henry Charles Albert David is born on September 15 in the Lindo Wing of St. Mary's Hospital in London; the three-month-old prince is christened by the Archbishop of Canterbury in St. George's Chapel in Windsor Castle.

1989

Joins William at Wetherby School, a pre-preparatory school.

1992

Joins William at Ludgrove School; Charles and Diana officially separate; Diana drives to Ludgrove to tell Harry and William the news.

1996

Charles and Diana's divorce is finalized.

1997

Diana is killed in a horrific car crash in Paris; Harry visits South Africa with his father.

1998

Joins William at Eton College.

2001

After Harry is caught drinking underage and smoking pot, Prince Charles takes him to meet recovering drug addicts at Featherstone Lodge, a drug rehabilitation facility.

2003

Graduates from Eton; begins his gap year and visits Australia, where he works as a jackeroo in the outback, and Lesotho, where he works with orphans and is so moved by them that he later produces a documentary about their plight, *The Forgotten Kingdom: Prince Harry in Lesotho*.

2004

Harry is photographed taking a swing at a photographer outside a London nightclub; visits Argentina, where he spends several weeks working on a polo ranch; begins on-and-off relationship with Chelsy Davy.

2005

Is publicly condemned for wearing a Nazi uniform to a costume party at the home of a friend; serves as a witness, along with his brother, during his father's wedding to Camilla Parker-Bowles; enters the Royal Military Academy Sandhurst for forty-four weeks of training.

2006

Completes training at Sandhurst and is commissioned as a second lieutenant in the Blues and Royals of the Household Cavalry Regiment; joins with Prince Seeiso of Lesotho to found the charity Sentebale to help vulnerable children in Lesotho.

2007

The UK Ministry of Defense announces that Harry will accompany his regiment to Iraq, but the army later announces that Harry's deployment to has been canceled out of concern for his safety and that of his men; Harry helps plan and host a memorial concert and service to honor Diana's forty-sixth birthday and the ten-year anniversary of her death; late in the year he is deployed under a media blackout to Helmand Province in southern Afghanistan for military duty.

2008

Serves in Afghanistan for ten weeks before his cover is blown by the media and he is forced to return home; is promoted to lieutenant and awarded an Operational Service Medal for his service in Afghanistan.

2009

Begins training to become an Army Air Corps helicopter pilot; spends eighteen months learning to fly the Apache attack helicopter; along with William, launches the Foundation of Prince William and Prince Harry.

2011

Is promoted to captain; takes part in Walking with the Wounded fund-raising expedition to the North Pole; serves as best man at wedding of William and Kate Middleton; briefly dates Florence Brudenell-Bruce; spends time in the United States for further helicopter training.

2012

Completes his Apache helicopter training; makes his first official royal visit on behalf of the queen, visiting Belize, the Bahamas, and Jamaica; is deployed to Helmand Province is Afghanistan as an Apache pilot.

For More Information

Books

Editors of *Life*. *The Royals: An Illustrated History of Monarchy—from Yesterday to Today*. New York: *Life*, 2010. This book portrays members of the royal family throughout history, including Prince Harry, in pictures and in text.

Editors of *Life*. *Diana at 50*. New York: *Life*, 2011. This book chronicles the life and death of Diana Spencer. Includes information about and numerous photos of her two children, William and Harry.

Andrew Marr. *The Real Elizabeth: An Intimate Portrait of Queen Elizabeth II*. New York: Holt, 2012. An in-depth look at the life and royal duties of Harry's grandmother, Queen Elizabeth II.

Joann F. Price. *Prince William: A Biography*. Santa Barbara, CA: Greenwood, 2011. This thorough biography of Prince William also includes in-depth information on Prince Harry and the rest of the royal family.

Periodicals

Jean Hannah Edelstein. "Republican Prince Harry Fanciers, Don't Be Ashamed." *Guardian* (Manchester, UK), March 7, 2012.

GQ. "Prince Harry Is Walking with the Wounded." March 29, 2011.

Kate Mansey. "Prince Harry Looks to Uncertain Future." *Australian*, March 12, 2012.

Tom Phillips. "After Running with Usain Bolt, Sporting Harry Takes to Rio's Beaches for Racing and Rugby." *Observer* (London), March 10, 2012.

Liz Raferty. "Prince Harry Charms Jamaican Hotel Staff." *People*, March 9, 2012.

Telegraph (London). "Prince Harry in Afghanistan: In His Own Words." February 9, 2012.

Internet Sources

Tom Gardner. "That's Their Boy! As Harry Charms the World, Just Look Who He's Taking After." *Daily Mail* (London), March 9, 2012. www.dailymail.co.uk/femail/article-2112893/Prince -Harry-charms-world-Jamaica-takes-Princess-Diana-Prince -Charles.html#ixzz1ovipRRj5.

Nick Hopkins. "Prince Harry in Afghanistan: PR Dream or Logistical Nightmare?" *Guardian* (Manchester, UK), February 9, 2012. www.guardian.co.uk/uk/2012/feb/09/prince-harry -afghanistan-analysis.

Gordon Rayner. "Prince Harry in Afghanistan: Royal Brothers on Frontline for First Time." *Telegraph* (London), February 8, 2012. www.telegraph.co.uk/news/uknews/theroyalfamily /9069631/Prince-Harry-in-Afghanistan-Royal-brothers-on -frontline-for-first-time.html.

Sky News. "Prince Harry Raced to Help Mugged Friend." December 18, 2011. http://news.sky.com/home/uk-news/article /16132647.

Telegraph (London). "Prince Harry: Proud to Be Named Walking with the Wounded Patron." February 10, 2012. www.telegraph. co.uk/news/uknews/prince-harry/9074772/Prince-Harry- proud-to-be-named-Walking-with-the-Wounded-patron.html.

Websites

Henry, Prince of Wales, NYTimes.com (http://topics.nytimes. com/topics/reference/timestopics/people/h/prince_harry/index .html). This page on the *New York Times* website provides links to a collection of noteworthy news articles about Prince Harry, as well as outside links.

Official Website of the British Monarchy (www.royal.gov.uk). This site contains extensive information on the entire royal fam- ily, including biographies, photos, links, and news stories.

Prince Harry, *People* (www.people.com/people/prince_harry/ biography). This site, hosted by *People* magazine, contains a wealth of information on Harry, including a biography and numerous links to news stories about the young prince.

Prince of Wales (www.princeofwales.gov.uk). The official website for Prince Charles. Contains a section on the Foundation of Prince William and Prince Harry as well as a section on Harry, with a biography, news, photos, and several links.

Sentebale (www.sentebale.com). The official website of the charity cofounded by Prince Harry and Prince Seeiso of Lesotho. Contains news stories, information on events, videos, newsletters, and much more. Also contains the documentary *The Forgotten Kingdom*, produced by Harry.

Picture Credits

Cherese Cartlidge holds a bachelor's degree in psychology and a master's degree in education. She has published numerous books for children and young adults, including biographies of Neil Patrick Harris, Beyoncé Knowles, Jennifer Lopez, and Taylor Swift. Cartlidge lives in Georgia with her two children.